THE CHRISTIAN FAITH EXPLAINED IN 50 LETTERS

THE
Christian Faith
Explained
IN *50* LETTERS

GERHARD LOHFINK

Paulist Press
New York / Mahwah, NJ

Cover image by badahos/Shutterstock.com
Cover and book design by Lynn Else

Originally published as Gerhard Lohfink. *Der christliche Glaube erklärt in 50 Briefen.* Copyright © 2018 Verlag Herder GmbH, Freiburg im Breslau, Germany.

English translation by Christopher Groß. Copyright © 2022 by Paulist Press, Inc.

Library of Congress Cataloging-in-Publication Data
Names: Lohfink, Gerhard, 1934– author. | Gross, Christopher (Translator), translator.
Title: The Christian faith explained in 50 letters / Gerhard Lohfink.
Other titles: Christliche Glaube erklärt in 50 Briefen. English.
Description: New York : Paulist Press, [2022] | English translation by Christopher Gross.
Identifiers: LCCN 2021003799 (print) | LCCN 2021003800 (ebook) | ISBN 9780809154784 (paperback) | ISBN 9781587689635 (ebook)
Subjects: LCSH: Catholic Church—Doctrines—Miscellanea. | Theology, Doctrinal—Popular works. | Christian life—Catholic authors—Miscellanea. | Faith.—Miscellanea.
Classification: LCC BX1754 .L585 2022 (print) | LCC BX1754 (ebook) | DDC 282—dc23
LC record available at https://lccn.loc.gov/2021003799
LC ebook record available at https://lccn.loc.gov/2021003800

ISBN 978-0-8091-5478-4 (paperback)
ISBN 978-1-58768-963-5 (e-book)

Published by Paulist Press
997 Macarthur Boulevard
Mahwah, New Jersey 07430
www.paulistpress.com

Printed and bound in the
United States of America

Contents

Preface...ix

Acknowledgments xi

Letter 1: How Faith Happens 1

Letter 2: From Animal to Human.......................................5

Letter 3: Stretched Out to Infinity 11

Letter 4: The Infinite God 15

Letter 5: Creation Out of Love...24

Letter 6: Ongoing Creation 29

Letter 7: God's Way of Revelation 32

Letter 8: Where Suffering Comes From............................37

Letter 9: Abraham, Father of the Faith 44

Letter 10: Why Israel? 49

Letter 11: Exodus Out of Egypt 52

Letter 12: Death in the Sea of Reeds.................................56

Letter 13: The Social Order of Mount Sinai......................60

Letter 14: Anchoring Human Rights 66

Letter 15: Rebellion in Israel...70

Letter 16: Jesus, Entirely Out of Israel 75

Contents

Letter 17: Jesus, Entirely from God 79

Letter 18: Jesus, God's Presence in the World 83

Letter 19: The Claim of Jesus 87

Letter 20: Can One Single Person Redeem the World? 92

Letter 21: Jesus's Death—A Sacrificial Death? 98

Letter 22: Jesus's Resurrection from the Dead 104

Letter 23: The Appearances of the Risen Lord 111

Letter 24: Jesus's Presence in the Holy Spirit 115

Letter 25: The Mystery of the Triune God 121

Letter 26: The Church Year 130

Letter 27: What Is Meant by *Church*? 135

Letter 28: The Power of the Sacraments 140

Letter 29: Admission into the Church 147

Letter 30: Strengthened through the Holy Spirit 153

Letter 31: Table Community with Jesus 158

Letter 32: Repentance and Healing 164

Letter 33: Salvation for the Sick and Dying 169

Letter 34: Acting with the Authority of Jesus 173

Letter 35: Symbol of God's Faithfulness 177

Letter 36: Life from the Sacraments 182

Letter 37: Life from the Holy Spirit 185

Letter 38: Life from the Commandments 189

Letter 39: Life Out of Prayer 193

Letter 40: The Our Father 197

Letter 41: "Glory Be to the Father" 202

Contents

Letter 42: The Communion of Saints 205

Letter 43: What Comes after Death? 211

Letter 44: Face-to-Face with God....................................215

Letter 45: Judgment...218

Letter 46: The Mercy of the Judge..................................221

Letter 47: United with the Risen Lord............................224

Letter 48: Creation Fulfilled 227

Letter 49: The Meaning of Easter....................................232

Letter 50: The Daring of Faith 236

Glossary 239

Preface

*I*n my childhood and even during my adolescence our parish Church was filled right down to the last seat during Sunday Masses, of which there were three on every Sunday morning. Otherwise all the parishioners would not have found a place in Church. Today the same Church sees only one single Mass on Sundays, and this holds equally true for many other congregations. Yet it is not just that the congregations are shrinking but also that much that had been customary in the past is crumbling. Being a Christian no longer constitutes a form of life, even for many of the baptized. To many others the question of God and the Church has become meaningless. Strangely enough, though, the numbers of those asking anew about the Christian faith keeps growing. They want to get to know it better. They want to know what Christian really stands for. As I have encountered more and more people in recent years asking about the Christian faith, I am venturing out to write this book.

I have opted to express, in letter format, what I want to say, to avoid as far as possible the format of a "treatise." In doing so, I am writing to a fictitious family. This does not, however, preclude the possibility that this book also contains letters I have addressed to real people.

Obviously, much more could be said about the Christian faith, and I have had to be selective. It still remains my hope that these fifty letters can convey the key elements, though I am fully aware that books cannot teach you how to be a Christian. This requires, above all, coming together with fellow Christians to stand together and for one another in Christian community. It is my heartfelt wish for all my readers to find and live in such community.

With deep gratitude, I dedicate this book to my Polish translator, Dr. Eliza Pieciul-Karmińska, professor at Poznań University.

Gerhard Lohfink
Munich, January 2018

Acknowledgments

*T*his book has been a strange undertaking because there never was a family Westford, and yet there is! Not only because there are many such life paths, but also for one other reason. The longer I wrote the letters to the Westfords, the more real and alive this family became to me, above all nine-year-old Anna. Sometimes I really worried for the three of them; mostly though they were a source of joy for me.

I owe the realization of this book to Carmelita and Gerd Block, Kristina and Johannes Hamel, Peter Zitta, Alessandro Perego, and my brother Norbert. All of them contributed their ideas at stages, but above all their interest in the book project helped me in my writing. Mr. Pachner was once again a highly reliable aid in obtaining the relevant literature sources. Dr. Bruno Steiner from the Herder publishing company encouraged and advised me time and again. Ms. Antje Bitterlich revised and corrected the manuscript with her characteristic thoroughness.

My special thanks go to Rev. Mark-David Janus, CSP, PhD, who included the book in the publishing program of Paulist Press, the loyal aid of Ms. Francesca Bressan from the license department of the Herder publishing company, as well as to Mr. Christopher Groß, who displayed such linguistic and theological sensitivity for the English translation.

Terms of significance for the Christian faith that might be unfamiliar to the unacquainted are covered in the text itself where possible. Where this is not feasible, the glossary at the end of the book provides an explanation for terms that are marked with an asterisk (*).

Letter 1

HOW FAITH HAPPENS

Dear Paul,

Your request that I help acquaint you and your wife with the Christian faith initially caused me a sleepless night. It kept me awake, as I could see nothing but trouble. Am I capable of this? After all, faith is more than a package of information to be forwarded just like that. At the same time, your request also tempted me. Can one imagine anything better than discussing the rationality and beauty of the Christian faith? With this letter, then, I accept this challenge and I will try my best.

The fact that we live so far apart, you in the North and I far down South, need not work against us. The internet gives us ample opportunities to bridge such distances speedily. For the moment, though, I prefer to stick to longer letters, as this format requires us to keep things (relatively) short but still allows us to make concise and reasoned statements. This will force me to address a specific aspect of the faith in a few pages. You, in turn, should speak frankly about your questions or difficulties. Meeting for longer exchanges could naturally become meaningful at some point, but for the moment, let's try letters first.

What is the Christian faith all about? You'll instantly notice that there is an all-dominating tension. It addresses the Highest there is: God. And one cannot speak about God the way one talks about any other "issue." God is holy, hidden, and unfathomable. God is not the world. (The world was created by God, but God himself is not the world.) That is one aspect.

On the other hand, the Christian faith is very much about the world and very concrete issues. It addresses both the larger and smaller things of our very real life. Anything and everything we do always touches upon the faith and is formed by it. Faith is more than a support, more than an aid in emergencies. It is a way of life.

We must bear and uphold this principal tension between the invisible God, before whom all our words and concepts fail us, and the real, visible world that makes up our life. God is not the world, and yet God wants our world. God is unfathomable, yet we need to talk about God with the words we take from our encounter with the world.

Closely tied to this principal tension is the notion that we cannot will ourselves to have faith. It must be granted to us as a gift. We cannot bring it forth out of ourselves. It is a gift; it is grace.

Yet, whenever someone finds faith, fellow humans always play a role. As for me, my parents were strong in their faith, and I do not know whether I would ever have found the faith without them. Moreover, at the crossroads in my life I encountered believers whose faith I felt and who showed me how it would be possible to live as a Christian. Then there were books that guided me to a deeper understanding of the faith. These books had not dropped from the heavens but were written by humans.

Put differently, this means that faith comes from God, but is conveyed to us by humans.

This becomes clearest with Jesus. He comes wholly from God, while he is still truly human, formed out of the history of Israel*. He proclaims the word of God, and yet this word comes entirely from human words. Such is the span, the tremendous and prolific tension, over which the Christian faith stretches.

Finally, let me address the issue that made you send your letter! A few months ago, your nine-year-old daughter Anna told you that she wanted to receive her first communion* together with other girls from her class. If I understood your letter correctly, you yourself are not baptized. Your wife is baptized and received confirmation but thereafter lost all contact with the Church. Suddenly, you are confronted by your daughter's wish, and you were both wise enough to not try to talk her out of it.

Such a wish by a nine-year-old would be easy to explain as the desire to share and join in the action of her friends. At the same time, a healthy portion of curiosity also comes into play, an inquisitiveness for the strange "other." Probably the white dress that girls still often wear for first communion also played a role. Psychologists could list a multitude of motives, some of which may not even be wrong. You and your wife, however, did not just give in to such psychological reasoning, nor did you tell your daughter, "Come on, this will pass!" Instead, you handled her wish gently and respected it, as you write, "We don't know what really goes on within her, and we did not want to break anything."

Here you have that very tension I mentioned earlier. You could explain the wish your daughter put before you as something very normal and natural. That's how life runs its course. God, on the other hand, acts precisely through such human affairs. You and your wife were open to the possibility of something greater, something over which one

3

cannot decree and that one must not touch. It was the very reason you wrote to me. You did not want to take away anything from your daughter, knowing at the same time that the entire issue also affects you.

Anna attended preparatory lessons for baptism, was baptized, and shortly afterward received the first communion together with some of her friends from school. You noted, "They were both two very nice days, solemn and still festive. My wife and I saw a new side to our daughter that we had not known before: a resoluteness and great earnestness, both of which touched us profoundly. As Anna bent her head over the baptismal font, tears welled up in my wife's eyes."

All of this has been working within you, and you do not want to leave Anna alone here. You do not want your daughter to cherish something that you yourself hardly know. It is far more than that. Maybe you even want to share the same path that Anna is now joyfully setting out on.

Your daughter's path reveals how faith can happen. It is all very human, with no voice calling from the heavens or a totally new world suddenly opening. Nor does the old world have to crumble. And yet, something new is coming our way, something we had never reckoned with. God can reach us in the most varied ways. Faith comes from God alone but is always conveyed through humans. And faith comes with a history. It starts somewhere, often somewhere seemingly insignificant, and suddenly the unexpected happens and it becomes quite exciting.

On second thought, I am rather glad about that sleepless night. I am even grateful to the two of you. You put me in a spot where I had to engage with what is happening in your family. It will do me good as well. With such gratitude, I greet you and your wife with all my heart.

Letter 2

FROM ANIMAL
TO HUMAN

Dear Paul,

Many thanks for your friendly answer, which I felt
came straight from the heart! As you and your wife
wholeheartedly agree with my proposal, let's begin with
letters. As you noted, you want to do more than just read
my letters, and as your job requires constant research, you
did just that and looked for "faith." Searching the internet,
you found that holy communion meant "giving and
receiving the gifts of bread and wine, which represent the
body and blood of Christ." Now you are asking yourself
what "blood" and "represent" are meant to signify.

Shall I address this question right now? I would
rather not just yet for the following reason. In my first
letter I mentioned God several times, noting that God is
holy, hidden, and unfathomable. This by itself was already
too much. I cannot simply begin to talk in a joyous and
freewheeling manner about God, and particularly the
Church's sacraments, without laying the groundwork. For
myself, I would want to look first at the world and the
human being, before addressing the subject of God. Our

project needs to begin with human beings. How are we to view them? What characterizes them? Are they just a highly specialized animal sporting a brain with more information storage capacity and denser neural networks than those of apes?

The twentieth century was still in its infancy when the founder of psychoanalysis, Sigmund Freud, posited the "three great humiliations of humanity." The first humiliation was Copernicus's insight that the Earth is not actually at the center of the universe. The second humiliation was Charles Darwin's discovery that humans are descended from the animal world, while the third humiliation is that a large part of the human soul's life escapes the reach of our consciousness. Things happen in our subconscious over which we have no power, so that we are not masters in our own house. Sigmund Freud's assertion was that these three revolutionary findings have shaken humanity to its core. They deeply humiliated human beings. No longer did they see themselves at the center of the world, separated from the animal kingdom, and masters of their own fate.

I must admit that to this day I fail to understand these three famous "humiliations." Never have I felt I was the center of the world, and I strongly doubt that our ancestors ever thought they were. Likewise, I am not shaken to find out that our planet Earth is but a dust particle in a huge universe. Rather do I marvel, when I look at outer space and am amazed that in its infinitely vast and ice-cold expanses, flooded by deadly radiation, that life as such is possible.

So what should we do with the abysmal spaces of the subconscious? Obviously, I am alarmed by dreams that well up in the night that tell me during my waking hours how many confused fantasies, fears of failure, and dark wishes occupy my soul. And I am saddened to realize during daytime that I keep doing things that I don't want to do. At the same time, I realize that I can keep myself from doing certain things, can rein in my fantasies, and that the wells of the subconscious bring forth not only convolutions but also necessities and beauty. Solutions flow forth for issues that had still seemed insoluble the day before, as well as affection, devotion, and gratitude. Why should I be humiliated by the sphere of the subconscious within me? After all, it connects me with the origins of humanity and the depths of the world. And are not these very depths the place where God can whisper quietly to me?

Moreover, why should I feel humiliated that human beings evolved in an arduous and highly complex process from the animal kingdom? I marvel at the incomprehensibly rich diversity of species I constantly encounter. There are the tiny blue flowers along the edge of the meadow whose name escapes me to this day; there is the unspeakably iridescent green of the beetle that recently crawled across my hand, the slinky gait of the cat crossing my lawn each morning, and even the common housefly that I dislike but whose take-off speed startles me whenever my hand wants to strike.

Should I really feel humiliated that God did not form humans from a lump of clay, as the Bible tells us in symbolic poetic condensation right at its very beginning? Or should I really feel humiliated that instead God set in motion an inconceivable evolution from organic compounds to macromolecules, to bacteria and algae, to jellyfish and amphibians, to the first land dwellers, to vertebrates and mammals, all the way to our apelike ancestors, and finally all the way to *Homo sapiens*?

In my previous letter to you, I noted how God acts through human beings. I need to expand on this fundamental theological insight by stating that God never interferes in the course of the world and history through *singular acts*. In history, God always acts through

7

human beings. In the procreation of life (just as in all other cases) God acts through so-called *secondary causes**: gases react and combine, molecules arise, initial cells with metabolisms and reproductive processes form themselves, all the way through to humanity, right through to your daughter, who is now doing her homework or playing in the garden.

Everything develops from a chain of "natural" causes, but the whole, from beginning to end, comes forth out of God's creative hand.

So, no! I cannot see this to be a humiliation of humankind or a degradation of God! A creation that God has so willed to unfold from the Big Bang to the mind of humankind is to me far greater and more admirable than humanity's cosmogonic myths of old. We should note, furthermore, that the story of creation narrated at the beginning of the Bible is no such myth. Instead, its theological precision demystifies archaic narratives, as it notes that the sun is no godhead and the moon no goddess but both are "great lights," which were created by God (Gen 1:16) and thus depicted with the methods of understanding nature *available at the time*.

I simply fail to take it as a humiliation that my skeleton, nervous system, digestive tract, and indeed my whole organism stem from far back in the beastly world, from where, over a process of millions of years, they evolved over many trials and countless errors.

I am equally aware that these very roots of humankind in the animal kingdom have caused many researchers to deny that humans are invested with mind and freedom. Their apparent free will was nothing else but mere imagination and self-deception. They claim that all human action is controlled by physical and chemical processes. Now I have nothing against these physical and chemical processes; they are omnipresent and ceaselessly at work, for without them, there would be no human life.

8

At the same time, such standpoints are careless simplifications. They are tantamount to equating a famous and fascinating painting with the question, "What is this painting? It is nothing more than a piece of canvas, stretched over some frame with dots and specks of color paint applied by brush strokes."

True, these facts and figures are valid and beyond doubt. But can they do justice to the picture? The painted artwork is decidedly more!

I could give an even better example. If everything we do is determined by purely physical and chemical processes, then we are nothing but puppets, biomachines, robots. Human affection, then, is wishful thinking; love, an illusion. However, we know all too well that the fascination of love is for the other person to turn to me out of their own free will. If their affection were nothing but control and coercion, it would be unbearable to me over time. You use a robot, but you don't love it.

Obviously, our days are not just filled with actions born out of free will. Most of what we do follows habitualized rules, is ritual and routine. The hour may come, though, when we must choose, and when we finally do, out of our own free will, from what has matured in many small incremental steps.

By the way, isn't it strange how those neuroscientists who consistently deny free will are most adamant that we adopt their viewpoint? "Let's stop this talk of free will!" says the neurophysiologist Wolf Singer! This is nothing but an *appeal* to us all, but such an appeal assumes prior freedom. Unless the sentence is meant to work like a magical irresistible incantation: "We should finally stop…" Is the scientist dressing up as a magician? We can see clearly that whoever denies free will invariably gets caught up in self-contradictions.

Dear Paul, it may well be that all of this is self-evident to you and your wife and that it does not bother either of you. You love your daughter, knowing that this love is more than animal instinct or hormonal governance.

Likewise, you love one another, wishing that this love is not controlled by hidden compulsions but based on free affection. Such a mindset is profoundly human, indeed Christian. The Church has always thought highly of human beings as it states, Human beings are loved by God and they are free to answer this love.

This free ability is the ultimate goal of all evolution and the final destination of an infinitely long way, which started out with the primal blue algae through to the loving eyes through which your wife and your daughter Anna see you. Best wishes to the three of you.

Letter 3

STRETCHED OUT TO INFINITY

Dear Paul,

Thank you very much for your reply and for directing me toward that experiment you had heard about. I searched the internet and quickly found what you referred to. It went as follows:

In 1931, the American psychologist Winthrop Kellogg started an experiment that he had thoroughly prepared and considered at length. He let a seven-month-old chimpanzee, Gua, live with his family to be raised with his ten-month-old son, Donald. The two infants were treated equally in everything from bathing, clothing, kisses, affection, highchairs, strollers, and so forth, because Kellogg wanted to know if the young chimpanzee would adopt human habits such as table manners or would learn at least a rudimentary form of human speech. However, the experiment took a different turn than what the professor had expected.

Although the ape infant adjusted half-heartedly to its environment, the real adaptability was evident with Donald. Though his speaking skills progressed alarmingly slowly, he had soon mastered the chimpanzee's grunt for food. Like Gua, he would beg for oranges in guttural gasps. His climbing dexterity exceeded that of all peers in the vicinity, and he preferred to move about on all fours, even though he could already walk. He would collect objects with his mouth and lick up leftover food from the floor.

The day he started to chew on his shoes, his father had seen enough and terminated the experiment (the mother never was too keen on the experiment in the first place).

What happened next? Once Gua had left the house for a zoo, Donald very quickly caught up what he had missed in his development. Later he earned a PhD in medicine, but he took his own life after his parents' death.

What does this story tell us? That it is a lot easier to train a human to monkey around than to turn an ape into a human? Seriously, though, it seems as if the human being is invested with something that sets him fundamentally apart from all animals. The stages of human development cannot be followed by animals. The process of becoming a human cannot be emulated. So what makes a human being a human?

The use of tools does not single out humans, as this is also found with animals. Certain finches, for example, hold thorns in their beaks to poke around for food, and our own animal ancestors used stones to break open marrow bones.

Is it language? Communication signals are equally evident and widespread in the animal kingdom as is the passing on of information. I recall a clip from my school days during a biology lesson. It showed the waggle dance of the scout bees in the beehive. This dance informs other bees of a food source and indicates not only the direction of flight but also the distance.

Animals certainly demonstrate feats of intelligence, often even of an impressive nature, and higher-developed animals display attachment, fidelity, and even grief and mutual assistance in a division of labor. We cannot even fully preclude the possibility that some animals have self-awareness. So where is the difference, and how do humans distinguish themselves from animals?

Free will, which I have already addressed, is what sets them apart, and the difference is in thinking.

One fundamental element of thinking is the formation of concepts. We do not call the strange object we sit at and eat from "that there"; we call it "table." In this way we have formed a concept that includes countless objects of the same kind. That is an incredible feat, as an infinite number of objects that share common features and are still very different can be named using one single word. The whole undertaking gets even more daring if we use words to form descriptive sentences. Such as "This is a table" or "This table is round" or even "Tables, chairs, and wardrobes are furniture." This capacity for abstract thinking presupposes that the human being can see a concrete object, some "that," against an infinite horizon.

This infinite horizon is evident in much more, as humans establish numerical systems, start to calculate, and work with series of numbers that stretch into infinity. The human being constantly longs for something new that he must have. After weeks of possessing it, he turns his attention to the next object, which is added to the heaps of objects already building up. Forever reaching out for something novel, new experiences, unconquered realms, human beings greedily sniff out the unknown and adventurous. This longing drives them to other lands and across the seas, the annual vacation not spent at home but on an island in the Caribbean. Their inquisitiveness is never quenched; their spirit of discovery constantly brings forth new explorative ventures and entirely new scientific fields.

Humans have the ability to question truth, not by appearance, by allegation, by desirability, but by what *is*.

In addition, humans can want what is good. Not what someone would just like, what would be agreeable and pleasant, but what is appropriate, objectively suitable and fitting, simply what is good.

Humans long for infinity; they are geared toward endlessness. Cows are satisfied with grass from the pastures. They do not admire or even care about the stars in the skies, while human beings marvel at them. They name them, send out space probes to explore Jupiter, the biggest planet in our solar system. Humans question everything, forever asking, Who, What, How, When, Why, Whether, Whence, What for?

This urge for the infinite is also evident in the phenomenon of art. What distinguishes a poorly painted picture, which you look at and immediately forget, from one you can see every day and never tire of? Seemingly, paintings you never can get enough of reveal something endless. Likewise, the pull that concerts have on many people. Obviously, there is not just music that awakens much in us and resonates in us; there is also music that generates something infinite and absolute. Why do human beings pray? We have prayed across all centuries, eras, and cultures. Just when we're in need? Just to lament? Just to beg? Or maybe also because humans want to reach out for the infinite? Toward the end of the fourth century AD, the great theologian St. Augustine said this in his *Confessions*, which is really one long prayer: "You have made us for yourself, O Lord, and our hearts are restless until they rest in you."

Our lives surely know many moments of restlessness that we would prefer to do without. But there is also a restlessness that corresponds with Augustine's words. Maybe Anna's wish to celebrate first communion* is ultimately, very quietly and unnoticed by her, borne out of that longing that is anchored deep within us and makes our hearts so restless. Heartfelt greetings to you all!

Letter 4

THE INFINITE GOD

Dear Paul,

You asked me to write about God in more detail, as I keep mentioning the word and seem to assume God is self-evident. You are right: It is time to speak about God. This does not mean, though, that I will tell you how to imagine God. We cannot, and if we try, what we conceive of is not God.

Is that so bad? I would say it is a good thing. God is so infinitely greater than all our imaginings. A God you could picture precisely would be a small idol, utterly distinct from the real God. Christian theology is right to say that one cannot decree or dispose of God, which in turn means that God is inconceivable and beyond our grasp.

In Christian art, of course, there are images and sculptures depicting God the Father. I do not know when these renderings began, probably as early as the Middle Ages. However, there are also medieval manuscripts that will not depict God but merely show his hand at the top edge of the page. To me that seems far better, as I have been quietly battling with all images of God for many years now. Most of them repulse me, and even the Sistine Chapel's famous fresco of Adam's creation fails to do justice to God. This airborne male with his well-groomed, gray beard and trained muscular arms leaves me cold.

I appreciate the compulsion Christians have had to depict God the Father. Theologically, however, this is not without problems. The Gospel of John, the youngest of the four Gospels, has Jesus say at one point, "Whoever has seen me has seen the Father" (John 14:9). This means that Jesus is God's perfect presence. Whoever hears Jesus hears God, and whoever sees him sees God. Whoever wants to know who God is must look at Jesus. He is the lasting and unsurpassable definition of God. Whoever wishes to imagine God should refrain from trying and instead contemplate Jesus in the Gospels. That will suffice.

What I am saying is that we should not want to *imagine* God, as these attempts will always fail. However, this does not mean that we should not *think* of God. To "think of God" is something totally different. If the Christian faith says God is eternal, infinite, and unfathomable, or when it says God is all-present and all-knowing, or that God is almighty, holy, just, and merciful, then this is *thinking* about God in terms and concepts that break through and transcend our own conceptions.

Christian theologians have always been intensively occupied by the question of whether it is possible to speak about God, and if so, how. They all agree that if we *think* of God, the terms and concepts we use are unlike those we deploy in our everyday life.

If I say, for example, God is "almighty," I do so by necessity from my own experience of "might" and what I mentally associate with it. I recall the might and power of nature, the power of the state, and the powerful sway charismatic people can hold, the power of magnificent poetry, the power of music and of love.

I invoke the "powers" at work in our world that can elicit remarkable or terrifying outcomes. However, I will then have to negate all these concepts of might and power and say that God's "might" is something different. This dissimilarity is unimaginably greater than any similarity. Ultimately, any talk about God will always be in negations of human experience. Though I must *start* from human experience, I must add that it is completely different with God!

A second example has me saying God is "just," to be followed up immediately by noting that God's justice is infinitely wider and hence totally different from any human justice. God's justice is at the same time pure mercy.

A third example: The Christian faith says that God is "eternal." Yet what is *eternal?* When we say "eternal," we involuntarily imagine an infinitely long timeline with no beginning or end. Can that really be God's eternity? This kind of eternity would be nothing but an infinitely long time, but as God is beyond all time, his eternity must also be something different, something inconceivable to us.

Every theology that seeks to think of God is, correctly understood, a *negative* theology. All it can ever say is that God is precisely not this or like that. So I ask again: Is that so bad? To me it is liberating because this *negative* theology guards us against false images of God. It saves us from stitching together a God as we would like to have him and misuse him for our own ends. How often have people been murdered in the name of God! Not only during the "Christian" Middle Ages, but in our times as well. To this day, fanatical "warriors of God" murder other human beings in the name of "God's will." Therefore, it is good that theology should sharply criticize and question all false concepts of God.

Having come this far, a serious question arises: How is this addressed in the Bible? Doesn't God speak like a human being in the Bible, feel like a human being, act like a human being? At the very opening of the Bible, in the Book of Genesis, God forms Adam from the dust of the earth's soil, breathes the breath of life into his nostrils before taking a stroll in the Garden of Eden in the evening breeze (Gen 2:7; 3:8). The whole Bible speaks of God as if God were a human. God rejoices or wells up in anger, turns toward or away from humanity, blesses or curses. How are we to reconcile this with my statements about negative theology? Why is the Bible entitled to anthropomorphize God in such ways?

These anthropomorphisms are contingent on the fact that we can only ever speak about God in metaphors. We can only ever talk of God in metaphors or parables, or we must remain silent. Long sections of biblical narrative are *metaphorical*. The Bible is fully aware of this, so that often it drives out one metaphor with another. It juxtaposes one with a second, which relativizes the first. For example, this is what happens in the Book of the prophet Hosea. In that book God's just wrath suddenly transforms into mercy, as we read, "For I am God and no mortal, the Holy One in your midst, and I will not come in wrath" (Hos 11:9).

Here the Bible itself rejects any anthropomorphisms of God but still speaks of God in "human terms." There is another reason for this as this is the only way the Bible ensures God is a "person." For God is precisely not "the Divine," not some kind of "primary cause of the world" or "oscillation of nature," and certainly not a "dynamic field of energy" as invoked so enchantingly by today's esotericists. God is a "person."

When we speak of the *human being* as a person, we speak of an inimitable "I," the unexchangeable and irreplaceable individuality, the unique, indivisible, and free self, which in this form has never been before and will never come again. Obviously, this concept of personhood, which crystallized from contemplating humankind, needs to be critically questioned, expanded, and transcended when applied to God. All the same, God is a real "vis-à-vis" us, with a "face" that "looks at us." God "sees" our need,

18

cannot "forget" us, "loves" us. When we speak about
God, then, we cannot help but use this anthropomorphic
language. Otherwise we would relinquish the "vis-à-vis,"
the "Thou" that God is to us. Or we would have to fall
silent over God. Having said this, we need to consider that
the images of God created in language are quite apart from
painted images or those in movies. Linguistic imagery is
more abstract than painted images. Linguistic metaphors
are more suitable and amenable to theology than film
sequences.

Dear Paul, so much for the question of how to speak
about God in the first place. It still leaves open the question
of whether God exists. Everything I have said so far does
not yet answer that. In fact, the question of whether God
exists cannot be answered in a few sentences.

Of course, I could refer to the long history of human
culture, the many people and multitude of religions, all of
which presuppose an existence of the Divine, of gods or
God. To the extent that we can survey history as such, the
fact that no people ever lived without religion should make
us pause. Every people knows of the "other," which you
open to, entrust yourself to, and which one must venerate
and worship. By the same token, "religion" dazzles us in
most varied and sometimes terrifying shapes and guises.

I therefore want to refrain from addressing religions
at this point, because I would then have to expand at length
on Israel's experiences with its God. But I shall leave that
for later when we come to address it in other contexts. This
letter merely wants to present you with one alternative.
May I ask you and your wife to imagine two very distinct
and different "views" of the world? I will outline these
viewpoints in the first person to make the exercise more
vivid. Imagine two people in conversation, the life of one
devoid of God, the life of the other governed by God.

The *first worldview* holds this: "I do not know where
the universe comes from. The world probably has always

existed, and science will know more about that someday. It is of no interest to me, though. My concern is how to live today. What I need is, above all, good health. It is of overriding importance and I will do everything for it. I also invest time and energy in professional training because I want to accomplish something meaningful. Of course, I also want to earn enough to afford a decent house and a carefree life. I want to get something out of life. Naturally, a family, as I don't want to live alone. I want to be together with others, be there for them, and hope that they will be there for me someday. I want peace and order for the world with right-minded states that provide justice and security. As I proactively support such a society, I joined a party with a program promoting human rights and environmentally friendly policies. We agree as a party that we must have 'values' that are recognized by as many as possible and that we will fight for these values. *Fighting*, though, is a big word and I don't like such big words. It is the small things that matter: courtesy, decency, listening, helping.

"Obviously, we need social justice and provisions for old age. I hope to age in peace and quiet. Of course, I will die one day, which doesn't frighten me as I have lived and loved. But it's all over some day, 'closing time' and curtain call. Nothing you can do about it. That's part of life. When I'm dead, it'll all be over for me. Hopefully, my kids can still live on in peace."

So much for the first worldview, or "reading of the world" if you want to call it that. Few would be as frank, but it exists and is widespread. Variations of this worldview abound, with some exercising excessively and idealizing gym membership. Others, in turn, devote their energy to animal welfare; others fight foreign infiltration through immigration. Many do not fight at all and just live each day as it comes. Some don't even consider their own passing, while others reflect on what they call a "dignified" departure from this earth. As said before, there are many different forms of this worldview, but despite their variations they share one thing: the complete renunciation of God. God plays no role in the lives of these people. They don't fight God; they are utterly indifferent toward God.

Let's now look at the *second worldview*, again in the first person: "I don't believe the world has always just existed, so to say, out of itself. Above all, it did not come about 'spontaneously' out of nothing. It is good for scientific research to progress continually and to work with ever more complex methods and models. Yet it has become blatantly obvious that the more questions scientists answer, the more new ones arise and the more uncharted territory opens up. An understanding of the world is only feasible if one believes in God as its creator. I am convinced that my life is not mere coincidence. God wanted me. God wants my happiness and wants history to thrive.

"Therefore, I want to give God my answer. I don't believe it is enough to hold 'values' that are consensually shared by society. Because God wanted and created the world, it holds a clearly ordered structure. The Bible's portrayal of humankind, above all, the Ten Commandments, reveals elements of this structure. 'Thou shalt not steal,' 'Thou shalt not commit adultery,' 'Thou shalt not commit murder'—these are not values that stand and fall because of society's approval. Instead, these (as well as all the other) commandments of God have their source in creation as willed by God. Furthermore, I love my family not only because they are my kith and kin but because they were given to me by God. I am fully aware that problems will keep cropping up in the form of different opinions, misunderstandings, and even rifts. At the same time, I know about mutual forgiveness and reconciliation, granted time and again by God. In addition, I work and stand up for a just society. I know that such a just and peaceful society should start within the Church, within the people of God. This is the actual place of world transformation. Finally, I am aware that death awaits me in the end. But death will not be the end. God is a God of life. In death I will finally meet God and nothing in my life will have been in vain. All my life will be assembled and resolved before God. Gathered before God with me and my life will be the entire history I shared with those close to me. In the end, injustice and violence will not prevail but hope and love will put things right."

Dear Beth and Paul, I have put before you two different worldviews, one devoid of God and one with God. I have tried to do justice to both, not wanting to demonize the one while praising the other to the skies. My purpose was simply to place before you two fundamentally different ways of thinking and living in this world.

Ultimately, how we want to live is our choice: either at the mercy of the ever-changing moods and spirits of the age or within clear structures of meaning, either in an absurd world that cannot answer any of the great questions of humanity or in a world whose answer lies with God, either in a world that is ultimately bleak and dreary or in a world invested with tremendous hope.

At least one thing seems apparent to me: without the assumption that God exists, the world loses its reason and, in the end, remains meaningless. Though evolution's ever-increasing complexity may have sparked humankind's lucid awareness and relentless search for meaning and happiness, this enlightened awareness runs mercilessly and incessantly into nothingness.

For when stripped of an answer to the primal human questions of "Why do I have to die?" and "Does final justice exist?" what becomes of the countless discarded, tortured, raped, murdered victims of history? The sufferings of innocent billions would then never be unearthed and resolved. This would degenerate the world into absolute self-contradiction, because even if there seemed to be many small islands of meaning, as a whole the world would turn into a ridiculous absurdity.

I am all too aware that there are so many more questions and things to say, but this letter has already become far too long. Alas, this is owed to the importance of the subject itself. I send both of you, and especially Anna, my heartfelt regards.

Letter 5

CREATION OUT OF LOVE

Dear Beth,

This time you wrote to me, and what a long letter it became. I am very grateful to you for it. You thought the two worldviews at the end of my last letter seemed somewhat artificial and that I had "constructed a pretty nice contrast." In reality, you think, it is a lot more complicated. You think there are many Christians who live almost as if God did not exist, while many non-Christians, who strive for the good, spend their lives in the search for truth and are therefore very open to God.

Then your letter expresses a big sigh. You wonder how nice it would be if Christians were to distinguish themselves from others because they truly lived their faith and their hope. How wonderful it would be if they did not display this apathy, this malevolent gossiping about others, this unending cantankerousness, all this repulsiveness that often makes our society so unbearable! Alas, the repulsiveness and unbearable traits are to be found among Christians as everywhere else. If Christians really led a different life, distinct from others, it might be easier to opt for the faith in God.

Now what can I reply? You have certainly raised an important, even vital aspect. The epistles in the New Testament*, especially Paul's letters, are full of admonitions directed at Christian communities. They challenge Christians to live what they have received. They should love one another with all their heart, help one another, and stand up for each other. They should forgive each other and requite evil with good. The fact that Paul and the other apostles keep reprimanding them shows that these admonitions were obviously necessary. They are just as necessary today, as so much of Christianity is in dire straits.

I could also use this moment to refer you to all the great and good things that have come to the world through the Church. I could refer you, above all, to the saints, as the Church has seen a large number of holy men and women whose example testifies what a life with God could look like and how Church is meant. There are still many such saints among us, but they are mostly hidden and unknown.

The point I wish to make does not follow this line, as I want to refer you to something completely different. Every church service opens with the assembled community confessing their guilt. Thus, we may hear,

> I confess to almighty God and to you,
> my brothers and sisters, that I have greatly sinned,
> in my thoughts and in my words,
> in what I have done and in what I have failed to do,
> through my fault, through my fault,
> through my most grievous fault....

If this classical confession is not spoken at the start of the service, the community will pray the Our Father* just before communion. In this prayer it asks God to "forgive us our trespasses, as we forgive those who trespass against us." What does that mean? If the community is not simply rattling off the words, it means that Christians live from and out of forgiveness. They are too aware that they are not much better than other people and that, time and again, they keep falling short of what they should really be and live. That is why they confess before God and before one another that they have sinned. Maybe this is even the one crucial aspect that sets them apart, because in our societies it is not customary to recognize and publicly admit one's own guilt, often for tactical reasons.

When Christians repeatedly confess their sins before God and one another, they reveal what it means to be Church. It is not primarily a congregation of the perfect and flawless, not a moral institution, where everything runs and works smoothly, but instead, it is a fellowship that lives out of God's forgiveness. The Church exists out of God's unmerited, gratuitous, and overflowing affection. The Church should be aware of this and should testify to it. And that is exactly the point I want to address in more detail in this letter, because I want to show that this unmerited and gratuitous love is already given with creation.

To illustrate my point, I will turn to the great Greek philosopher Aristotle, who lived four centuries before Christ*. For Aristotle, God is the infinitely perfect spirit. Since eternity, God has existed out of himself and through himself. God is pure spirit, purest thought, which for Aristotle is the highest there can be. Then the great philosopher wonders: If God is purest thought, what is God thinking? To which Aristotle replies, "God thinks himself."

To Aristotle, this is perfectly logical: What else should God think? After all, God is the perfect Being-in-itself. Were God to think of anything else but himself, such as human beings or any other object, God would no longer think about the most excellent and exalted. God would then move away from himself and lose his perfection.

Christian theology made free and grateful use of Greek philosophy, adopting countless terms and philosophical concepts from Aristotle for its own theology. At the same time, Christian theology went far beyond Aristotle, aware from the start that God is not just self-possession but pure and perfect love.

Dear Beth, grant me a comment on the side!

I have already used the word *love* numerous times in my letters, as I did just now and even in connection with God! One should refrain from using the word *love*, as it is constantly misused and terribly worn out. I fail to find another word, though, and cannot get past it.

Once more, then: God is not just self-possessing but pure love. Pure love, though, does not stay alone with itself. It wants to give freely; it wants to give away. It longs for a Thou, an other, whom it can love and to whom it can relinquish itself freely. That is the very reason why God created the world, a world that in a long evolution was to develop toward humankind. God wanted humankind—out of pure love.

God is not orbiting himself, is not perpetually and forever self-referential, but God thinks of the world. Thereby God calls the world into being so that the world may partake in his infinite, eternal life. The universe, the world, humans are created out of love. God wants and wills the creation, and he wants to elevate it up to God.

Dear Beth, this to me is one of the most beautiful mysteries of the Christian faith. It is so magnificently beautiful as it brings so much fittingly together. You are also experiencing how true love always expresses itself as going outside of yourself, reaching out to your husband, to your daughter, to others, to a sick neighbor. When we reach out to someone else in love, we give a little of ourselves, maybe even not a little but all of ourselves.

At the opening of its worship, the Christian community confesses that it has fallen short of being there for others, that everyone stayed with themselves and only thought of themselves. Despite all their failings, they pray and ask for God's love. And God gives it and renews us human beings in forgiveness. Kind regards!

Letter 6

ONGOING CREATION

Dear Beth,

Thank you very much for your answer and your husband's kind greetings. You told me so much about Anna this time, which I had so hoped for because in all honesty, I was curious to know whether baptism and first communion had changed anything in your daughter's life.

This seems to be the case as you can engage in more serious conversations with her than before. The biggest joy for me, though, was to read that Anna now attends Mass every Sunday with her best friend. At the same time, she told you that hardly anyone from her first communion class joins them anymore, which she cannot understand.

You spoke with your husband about this and both of you were stung by your daughter's sorrow. So you decided to join her for Mass on Sundays, even though this gets in your way occasionally. I will not make any grand statement about this, though I am quite sure that this is the biggest gift you can offer Anna.

Allow me now to continue with the topic from the last letter, in which I had written about the world's creation. God did not create the world out of some fancy or, to put it in even more humane terms, because God was in the mood for an experiment. It was created out of love, freely given and overflowing love. Now, love should not be taken as something that *must* give itself away. Love that is coerced is not free and hence is no longer love. Though God's love gives itself and thus hands itself over, it does so in complete freedom. Creation is therefore a gift *freely* given by God.

Nevertheless, we need to add one important aspect. I have already said repeatedly that God "created" the world. This is how it is almost always formulated. However, is it correct to use the past tense here? After all, this implies there was an act of creation "in the beginning" after which the world was finished. Yet, the world is far from completed and continues to revolve with an incredible dynamic force. The dust and gases from gigantic clouds of molecules still give birth to countless new stars. Galaxies still burst asunder, the evolution of biology continues unabated, technological progress keeps advancing together with all the questions it raises, and all of this with increasing acceleration.

Moreover, when we say that God once created the world, we are thinking of God within time. By speaking in this manner, maybe God created the world some 13 billion years ago, but God does not act within time. God acts out of the eternity that is his own, as time and space only come forth from the creation of the world. God, however, is absolutely beyond space and time. It is therefore wrong to say that God "created" the world. The entire history of the cosmos, the world, and humanity is one singular act of creation.

The fact that I am alive, that you, dear Beth, are alive, that your husband, Paul, and daughter, Anna, are alive and here is all part of this one single act of creation. Without God's love, which unceasingly calls us into existence, we would immediately fall back into nothingness. We "are" only because God loves us. There are plentiful reasons why

Ongoing Creation

Christians go to church each Sunday to celebrate Mass, but one is to thank God for continually giving us the gift of our existence.

The weather by me today is picture perfect for a Sunday: blue skies and a sprinkling of white clouds and the geraniums outside my window in full bloom. Hopefully you are enjoying the same fine weather. Kindest greetings to all of you!

Letter 7

GOD'S WAY OF REVELATION

Dear Paul,

Your letter takes up what I had said about creation and connects it with an extremely important development in our society. Today many people are committed to halting climate change, conserving the natural resources of life, protecting plant and wildlife, and, thank God, many also to protecting unborn life. Among Christian-minded people, but not only there, the world is about "preserving the integrity of creation." As you write, these issues are also important to you.

So they are to me. Every generation and era revolves around a center from which it thinks and feels. Or to put it differently, every age follows its mission and vision. In past ages, this vision for many pointed toward their homeland and their nation's honor, triggering senseless and criminal wars, some of which continue to this day. If only such ideas of nation were replaced by an awe and respect for life and creation, it would represent tremendous progress.

This would be all the more important as it could offer modern people an opening to God, because we must not do everything we can simply imagine, nor should we do everything we are capable of. Instead, we should treat carefully what we encounter and find given, namely, the structures of creation. We should learn to listen to what God wants to tell us through creation. I want to address this in more detail now. How does God speak to us human beings? How does God reveal himself to humans?

Obviously, it is not a voice from the heavens, nor does God speak out of a burning bush or with flashes of lightning and the roar of thunder coming down a mountain.

When the Bible uses these images, the texts mean to express, in symbolic condensation, what historically often took long and arduous paths of comprehension and insight. All these texts are true, but not superficially! They amalgamate the experiences of God, made in Israel over centuries, in telling imageries that are beautiful, valuable, and unsurpassable. Yet these images distill many long chains of experience into one narrative image.

I need to elaborate and go further by asking, "How is it possible for God to communicate with humans?" We already looked at humans' long developmental progress from the animal kingdom, the way human beings very slowly transitioned from a world of mere instincts into a world of freedom, and how gradually mind and reason awakened within them. Likewise, the progression toward the human experiences of God also stretched over very long periods.

We know nothing about such experiences among early hominids. Though we may assume that humans in the early Stone Age were grateful if they trapped a large animal or found a beehive full of honey, we may equally assume that they did not simply abandon their deceased but slowly accumulated knowledge of "powers" larger than themselves.

We should probably not yet call "God" the powers that transcended life and that became ever more noticeable during these early phases of humanity. Was the "Lord of Beasts" that was implored for hunting success and whose pardon was sought for the kill of the prey already a god in the sense of later high cultures? Was "Mother Earth," worshiped as the fount of all fertility among the first agrarian settlements, already a goddess?

Were the ghosts of the deceased, beseeched for help, feared for their wrath, and soothed for their mercy, already gods? In their attempt to describe the myriad expressions of early religions, cultural anthropologists and scholars of comparative religion struggle to find the right terminology.

We need not concern ourselves here with such details, but we can hold on to the crucial point that the emergence of religion was concurrent with the development of humans. With the progression of human culture, human experiences of God also grew more complex. Religions with elaborate systems of gods developed, as did such worldviews as those held by Buddhism that were devoid of all gods. Long before that, forms of religion developed that, at first glance, appear to be primitive but for whom modern research has shown we need to be extremely careful when we use the word *primitive*.

As noted above, we need not concern ourselves here with the concrete details of these developments of religion. My question is theological in nature: Has the true and only God revealed himself here already? Has God already shown himself in such constellations? Could such circumstances already yield insights into God?

The answer is that God suffuses all of creation with his spirit. In the Book of Wisdom, the Bible says, "The spirit of the Lord has filled the world" (1:7). We may read this to mean that God's love, which is behind all creation and carries and fulfills everything, wants to be recognized.

34

God's love is virtually urging us to encounter and start conversing with humans. This conversation begins wherever the mind of humans opens up, wherever they use their reason and take their first steps into freedom. This is a real conversation, as God reveals himself in the beauty of his creation, in need and joy, in all things, as he speaks through them the word of God's affection.

God wants to communicate, and humans want to hear. As we have seen before, in their minds, humans are stretched out to infinity, and to the extent that they open up, they can also hear. To the extent that they listen, they can also comprehend.

Naturally, the conversation between God and the human being is initially conducted clumsily by humans. Their mind and freedom need to mature first, so that the dialog, insofar as it refers to humans, is still hesitant, restrained and accompanied by misunderstandings over long stretches.

Even more, the awakening mind of humans keeps growing in potency and breadth and so can also refuse this dialog. People can close themselves off, can look away, and can contort or disfigure what was initially revealed as God's love.

In humanity's history, therefore, "religion" appears as an ambivalent and complex phenomenon. It brings forth devotion and veneration, the search for truth and longing for the good; it shapes and forms an entire life through being the totally other, which transcends human beings. At the same time, it begets the evil ugly face of religion wherever humans close themselves off from the dialog with God, whenever they seek to instrumentalize God or the gods for their own ends, and when they return to the animalistic in the name of the divine. This is where perversion sets in, where insight and recognition foster chaos, devotion turns to disgust, love becomes fear, and humility turns into violence.

Religion is two-faced. Folk religions have their own dignity as well as their limits. They are born out of necessity but are also doomed to failure. They were necessary preliminaries to a deeper understanding of God. Humans had to behold their self-made godheads first, before recognizing the true God through the denial of these idols.

Dear Paul, I am sure you can see what I am getting at here. From God's perspective, creation has always been filled by the Spirit, care, and love of God. How this manifests itself in concrete terms depends on humans and their freedom. We can open ourselves up to it, or we can refuse to do so. We can be all ears, or we can refuse to listen. We can stop and stay where we are instead of taking the next step toward recognizing God.

The uniqueness of Israel, of this tiny people wedged in between superpowers, was precisely that it dared to take this new step at a crucial moment. It opened to God entirely. The Bible consolidates this new step in the figure of Abraham*. The Bible rightly sees this step as taken by *one individual* because it is always an individual whose faith can stir the many to move. Abraham left his homeland, which needs to be translated as the overpowering religious system of his age, and put himself fully at the service of God. This step turned into an unthinkable history that theologians call the "history of revelation." My next letter shall cover Abraham and the significance of his story. Kindest regards to all of you.

Letter 8

WHERE SUFFERING COMES FROM

Dear Beth,

I had originally wanted to address Abraham this time, but my previous letter caused intense discussions between you and your husband. You both struggle with my talk of God's love, which I invoked repeatedly and above all in my last letter as so self-evidently a love that brings forth and suffuses all of creation. You ask how one is to square this "love" of God with the many catastrophes within creation and its immeasurable suffering. You question the earthquakes that destroy cities, the mudslides that bury hundreds of people, the hurricanes and tornadoes that plunge the poor even deeper into their misery, the diseases and pandemics that slay millions of victims, and everywhere in nature, ceaseless devouring and being devoured.

"The bird eats the worm, the cat chases the bird, and the dog chases the cat," you write before concluding, "What a creation!" You formulated your questions with fervor and a hint of saddened dejection. "How can it be," you ask at another point, "that God's apparently benevolent creation is so full of murder?"

I shall try to answer your questions and will start where matters are apparent. When we speak of murder, we speak of humans, as animals kill but do not murder. Only humans murder, whether it be out of envy, avarice, hate, or religious delusion. The unspeakable suffering that permeates all history is largely made by humans. Imagine a world without corruption, without war, without refugees, exploitation, quarrels, or conflicts that start in infancy and then subsume all areas of life. We would not recognize that world.

The suffering caused by the natural catastrophes would look different. If peace and solidarity ruled the world, we would not see people forced to settle in high-risk areas that are forever threatened by flooding, mud slides, volcanic eruptions, and earthquakes. Obviously, such an assertion has its limits. I am all too aware that many catastrophes are unpredictable and that plenty of human suffering would remain in the world despite all precautionary measures. Take, for example, only the recent catastrophes in India, where monsoon rains flooded huge swaths of land. You rightly also refer me to the countless diseases. Though these can also be self-inflicted, the terrible hardship that individual illnesses and epidemics can cause in the world cannot be argued away. Nor does it help to say that in these cases human reason and readiness to help could do a lot. We must drill deeper.

So I ask you this: Are birth and death, blossoming and withering, becoming and passing, indeed, even eating and being eaten within a lengthy food chain, not all part and parcel of life? In every second of our life, the microcosm of our body is a battleground of relentless slaughter. Our body is constantly under attack from alien pathogens, be they bacteria, viruses, fungi, or parasites, all of which are geared to conquer our bodies and attack our own healthy cells.

Our immune system must deal with this constant onslaught of microorganisms, to which end it sends out troops to fight, such as the immune cells. The pathogens in our body and the molecular counterforces are locked in a merciless battle. It is an endless frenzy of killing and feeding, without which our life would swiftly come to an end.

Even the inside of our mouth is the scene of unrelenting skirmishes. Anyone who thinks that his mouth is germ-free after brushing his teeth is deceiving himself. Over two hundred distinct species of microbes dwell in the mucous membranes between our lips and our throat. Only a minor portion of them is harmful. Most of these bacteria in our mouth maintain the health of our gums and teeth by acting as a kind of police force.

Here too we see unchecked voraciousness, ruthless battles, and ceaseless killings on a microbiological level. But without this unending war, our teeth would soon fall out! I don't even want to mention what goes on in our bowels. Today, we know what a healthy intestinal flora means, but this, too, only functions through the ceaseless destruction of cells.

I don't want to begin to count the astronomically high number of body cells that die off daily as part of a natural process and need to be flushed out so that our bodies can renew themselves continually. Specific genes ceaselessly trigger preprogrammed cell death. If our cells do not constantly die off but instead proliferate with life, we fall victim to cancer.

Dying is an integral part of evolution and thus of life. Life presupposes death. The very fact that we are alive and can breathe, that we are surrounded by the right atmospheric conditions, that our blue planet provides us with air and life-sustaining water all requires minute fine-tuning of the universe and constitutes an incredible balancing act of the cosmos. However, we need not be afraid of this persistent endangerment, of our life wedged amid death. It is indispensable to the miracle of life.

There would be no evolution without the constant death of living organisms, as evolution presupposes procreation, constant reproduction. Such reproduction, though, is possible only if *one* generation makes way for the *next*. Thus, the formula is that without death there is no generational succession, and without the succession of generations, no evolution.

I am convinced that these deliberations need to be taken one step further. Because without the succession of generations, there is not only no evolution, but without evolution there is no history. *Homo sapiens* follows from a long evolution, and once this point was reached, it did not stop. Biological evolution also unfolds in the evolution of civilizations and culture, because for a trained singer to sing "Celeste Aida" requires a highly sophisticated development of the human larynx but likewise the development of the art of opera all the way up to Giuseppe Verdi. Yet this development in operatic art is inconceivable without the totality of European history. All of this is inextricably linked to one another. It is really true that without evolution there would be no history!

Let me take this even one step further by claiming that without history the world would not know freedom. Does this make sense? Consider how we come to take truly free decisions in our life. Don't they just follow from others having given us these freedoms? Aren't all these freedoms that we enjoy as common citizens the legacy left to us by those who went before, with their fearlessness, resolve, and clear-sightedness? Without those individual freedom fighters with the pluck to speak the truth to tyrants, we would never muster up the strength to do so.

Our own freedom rests on those who walked before us and fought for these freedoms.

I consider the saying "No freedom without history" to be a fundamental dictum because freedom does not simply fall from heaven. It must be fought for, and it is transmitted to us through the life and courage of great individual human beings. Thus, freedom and liberty reach us through history, just as oppression and the lack of liberty do.

In this train of thought, allow me to take one last step and say, "No freedom without history, and without freedom no love." The highest good that life can hold is for one person to turn to another person, wholly and forever. However, this can happen only in freedom. Love must be free, otherwise it is not worthy of this name.

This is all meant to show that love presupposes freedom, freedom presupposes history, and history in turn presupposes evolution. Dying, however, is integral to evolution and therefore is nothing negative in itself. Nonetheless, one vital aspect needs to be considered as well. We do not simply live in a world that corresponds to God's will of creation. Instead, we inhabit a world infused and characterized by a long history of guilt and marked by a terrifying sequence of human refusal. You may recall that my last letter had said that humans can remain at a standstill or can progress. To the extent that they attain growth in mind and freedom, they can refuse to acknowledge God or open to God. Too often, humans have closed themselves off to the good and to freedom and with that, to God.

Regrettably, human history is not just resplendent with prudence, mutual help, and striving for truth, but equally marred by egoism, terror, crime, and denials of God. Heaps of human guilt have been amassed and obfuscate our view. We are born into a history that is everything but innocent. Where the entire world should reflect God's glory, it has long ceased to, and history's potential for guilt clouds our eyes.

The Church, incidentally, refers to this guilt potential and these structures of evil into which we are simply born without our own guilt as "original sin." The term may be a bad one, but the reality described by this extremely misleading word is one that surrounds us.

Due to the history of guilt that precedes us and the consequences of which we enter into, we often fail to recognize what creation actually is. The so-called scourges of nature such as catastrophes, illness, and death are part of the world, its finiteness and historicity. The history of human guilt and its residual waste have changed the quality of these "evil scourges." We no longer see them immediately on the horizon of a God-given dimension of meaning.

Thus, we do not see death as a path that brings us closer to God, but as the terrifying and tragic termination of our life. Nor do we experience nature as the multifaceted and colorful creation of God, but as an abysmal and highly dangerous nemesis of humans. To give you one last example: Don't we fail too often to see our fellow human beings as brothers and sisters standing at our side so that we might cooperate and help each other? Instead, we take them a priori to be our competitors and antagonists.

Nevertheless, none of this provides an answer to the question of whether creation is good. Probably every thinking Christian has asked himself why God did not create a totally different world. A world without evolution, without strenuously developing toward God, without the painful progression to our final end, and above all without human sacrifice. In other words, a creation that has reached its destiny straight away.

A perfect paradise with everything provided, a static world that knows no failure or sin? Maybe God got it wrong. Is the world so created by God maybe misconstrued, poorly constructed, a massive error?

The answer to all this can only be that in a world without evolution, without the laborious progression toward God, without the painful advancing toward our final end, freedom would not exist. In such a world we would be mere puppets, infantile, euphoric bio-machines hardwired for pleasure, as Aldous Huxley depicted them in his 1932 novel, *Brave New World*.

Freedom is an infinite asset, which alone makes humans into human beings, into admirers and lovers. Because only as free human individuals can we experience the joy of never-ending love.

Dear Beth! This letter has turned out frightfully long (with so much more left unsaid), and it did so once more, because the matter addressed is so significant. Yours was one of the key questions, querying the suffering in the world and asking about God's good creation. Is the creation really good? I could not ignore or sidestep this question, so please bear with me for making this letter so lengthy.

I greet you very warmly and wish that you, your husband, and your daughter, despite all the darkness and evil in the world, can also see the great and beautiful around us.

ABRAHAM, FATHER OF THE FAITH

Dear Paul,

I hope the two of you have digested the microbes and parasites of my last letter. I deliberately held back from adding the mosquitoes, spiders, scorpions, and snakes, or for that matter, the squirrels, nightingales, butterflies, swallows, and wild horses, because the world God gave us is wonderfully resplendent. The real problem is not subhuman creation but rather humans themselves. It is the long, drawn-out history, initiated with early hominids roughly two million years ago, that then began with the arrival of *Homo sapiens* approximately 300,000 years ago. It was a long history with only gradual gains of insights.

Looking over the full breadth of this history, one can say that human beings were capable of opening to God's eternal love. Humans were able to answer this love time and again and thereby managed to take the next step and become, in a deeper sense, more "human." Conversely, humans were also able to shut themselves off, falling back into the beastly. This, however, was no longer animal but human beastliness. Animals kill their prey; they cannot do otherwise. Humans have reached a point at which they could act otherwise but still kill their fellow humans. This is the moment when aberration, evil, sets in.

Add to this another element. To the extent that the mind and freedom grow in humans, they invariably beget "history," as this is the juncture at which memory and recollection begin. Recollection in turn brings the past back to the present.

What once was, always forces itself back into the present. It is not fully past or over, it keeps affecting the present. Thus, the good can be recalled and thereby preserved, and because it is so preserved, it can even grow. A whole culture of goodness, helpfulness, and solidarity can grow from it.

Likewise, evil can stay within the world in the same way. More still, it can accumulate, "potential" for evil can spring up, "force fields" and "concentrations" of evil can amalgamate. Let's call them simply "forces of evil." These evil forces always have their roots in the sins committed by individual humans and groups of humans. Because sin always begets consequences that fester in the world, these potentials for evil establish themselves, take on a life of their own, and thereby darken history.

My abstract narrative here is the same as the subject matter of the first chapters of the Old Testament*. These chapters illustrate very tellingly how evil grows in the world. It starts with humans shunning and ignoring God's quiet whispers, while other voices well up inside them. In the Book of Genesis these voices are personified with the image of the "serpent" (Gen 3:1). The serpent tempts humans to glorify themselves. Such self-glorification, though, logically triggers violence in the subsequent generation, as Cain kills his brother Abel (Gen 4:8). And so it continues, with one act of violence begetting the next act of violence. This accumulates into a history of evil, a potential for violence, a biosphere of evil, which culminates, as we read, in the earth being "filled with violence" (Gen 6:13).

The first chapters of the Bible certainly also know the other side of the story as they speak of people such as Enoch and Noah, who are open to God and go their life's path with God (Gen 5:24; 6:8). Overall, though, the Bible's portrayal of the world is as frightening as the world in which we live today. It is a world soaked and corrupted by violence, which even glorifies its aggressive brutality, as embodied by the figure of Lamech (Gen 4:23–24).

Thus, the violence described is not just singular acts or the brutality of individuals; instead, it is a history of violence begetting a sphere of doom and evil. One could compare this sphere of doom with the contaminated environment. Many contributed to soiling our environment and to polluting the world's seas with plastic waste. At first, we are born innocently into this environment, but soon we contribute toward contaminating the air, the soil, and the water. In much the same way, modern humans are born into a history that is already characterized by self-glorification, manipulation, and violence. In my last letter I had already alluded to this preexisting calamity into which we are born and in which we then invariably participate. The Church refers to this with the ambiguous term "original sin."

Evil exists in our world not only in individual acts but also as an accumulation, as accumulated power, as tenuous and long-lasting history spreading malice, much like a tumor begins to metastasize. Every human being inevitably enters this history, into these calamitous potentials, into this power of evil. The Bible is very frank in its sober description of the world the way it is.

Yet the Bible does not stop there. It takes this background to tell a counter-narrative. The start and at the same time the embodiment of this counter-narrative is Abraham. Though the historical Abraham remains very obscure for us, the biblical Abraham brings together and crystallizes Israel's experiences gathered over centuries. Abraham stands as the beginning of something new in history, while he simultaneously embodies this new history in all its breadth. To that extent Abraham is also our "father." What, then, is this new element?

What is new in Abraham is the way he fully opens to God. He is all ears; he is listening with all his might. He wants nothing other than what God wants. His unceasing listening to God brings him to "leave behind," to "exit," everything that was before. Abraham dares to take the step of leaving his homeland and his father's house. Just on the word of God, he sets out for a promised land he doesn't even know of. This is how the Bible tells the story:

"Now the LORD said to Abram*, 'Go from your country and your kindred and your father's house to the land that I will show you. I will make of you a great nation, and I will bless you, and make your name great, so that you will be a blessing. I will bless those who bless you, and the one who curses you I will curse; and in you all the families of the earth shall be blessed.' So Abram went, as the LORD had told him. (Gen 12:1–4)

Allow me to recall that these are all statements made about Israel. This is the path that Israel takes, condensed in the patriarchal figure of "Abraham." In that sense, Abraham really exists. He embodies Israel's exodus out of the religions. He stands for the beginning of something totally new in the world. Something that leaves behind everything that is mere religion and that leads to what we call "faith." Faith is counting on God. Faith means asking from God no longer what one wants for oneself but what God wants. Faith means to entrust oneself to God with all one is. Faith means to live from God's promises. Not alone and isolated, but together with a whole "people." In this sense Abraham is the "father of faith."

47

He is also "father" of our faith. Everyone who comes to faith embarks on Abraham's daring undertaking, leaving behind a great deal of what has kept you on your toes and preoccupied.

Everyone who dares to count on faith starts something new and enters a life-changing adventure, which will open a new land, a land full of promise. This "land" is not necessarily a territory, but it is a life space, a life form, a form of people being with one another and for one another.

Dear Paul, I realize this letter is getting too long again. So let me close in expectation of your questions, and heartfelt greetings to all of you.

Letter 10

WHY ISRAEL?

Dear Beth,

How nice that you and your husband are taking it in turns to write these letters. It appears to be your talent to be spot-on with your questions. The penetrating question you posed this time is why the "new" of which I wrote began in Israel of all places? Why not in China? Why not in Egypt, in Greece, or with the Maya in Central America? Why did it happen in that tiny and insignificant Israel, for which Abraham stands?

A first, albeit superficial, answer could be this: because Israel lies at the crossroads between Asia, Africa, and Europe, and thus at the intersection of such high cultures as the Assyrians, Babylonians, Phoenicians, and Egyptians, all with their impressive religious systems. It was precisely their "being in between the big religions" that allowed Israel and its theologians for centuries to contemplate, compare, differentiate, and criticize. This process of comparing and differentiating fed into Israel's experiences of God, which were then collated, condensed, continued, and constantly critically reviewed in the book we call the Bible. The "new" was thus also contingent on external factors and arose from a geographical and cultural constellation. Whenever God acts, secondary causes always come into play.

Obviously, this by no means explains it all. When you, dear Beth, got to know your husband, external contingencies certainly also had a role to play. It was a specific constellation as well as circumstances that you simply liked about your husband and that you certainly could name.

I am convinced you could easily list a few such factors straight away. And yet, over and above all of this, there remains an element one cannot name or explain. It is the innermost of what we call love. True love is the encounter of two freedoms and this conflation retains an inner sphere that cannot be resolved rationally. It remains an intimacy, indeed a mystery, and, hopefully so, for the rest of your lives.

All this holds equally true for the relationship between God and his people. I stick by what I said before about God's urgent love being directed at the whole world, in the same way as I stick to the statement that something new happens in the world wherever people open up to this love of God. By the same token, it remains a mystery of freedom that this new element should have happened in all its consequential might out of the encounter of God with this one particular people. The Bible calls it the mystery of "being chosen" and even terms it *love*.

This notwithstanding, one needs to add immediately that this is no love between two partners, who retreat as a pair and just revolve around themselves. Instead, this love opens far and wide. This love does not exclude the other nations but occurs for the sake of these other peoples. Abraham shall be a blessing to all nations (Gen 12:3), and that is why he leaves his father's house, his kith and kin, his people, and entrusts himself fully to his God. Anyone seeking to become a Christian enters this faith of Abraham and must dare to have the faith, trusting not to lose anything but only ever to gain. Such a seeker's life will be blessed and will become a great blessing for those immediately around and many others.

I greet you very cordially and wish you, Beth, your husband, and your daughter, Anna, that your heart may open up a little to this Abraham, to his daring undertaking, his faith, and the blessing that flows forth from him.

EXODUS OUT OF EGYPT

Dear Paul,

You wrote that you had a bit of a disagreement with your wife regarding the time of your courtship. Both of you took a trip down memory lane and recalled what you both liked in the other at the time. This brought up issues that you seemingly never had talked about. There were the "intelligent eyes," the "bright mind," and the "voice that was enchantingly soft and gentle," and then other aspects also surfaced. For example, how profoundly your wife was moved by the respect and trust witnessed in the dealings between your parents. The best thing, though, was that Anna was with you all the time during these recollections. She was all ears, listening to her parents reminiscing, and finally asked you, "What did you actually like about me?" Well, there were the "tiny little hands" and the "delightful small nose," all of which you recounted in good humor and which turned into a real profession of love to your daughter.

Let's now return to Abraham and how he reflects Israel's long history. The Bible's narrative records key moments and crucial situations from this history. It does so to show Israel's trials and errors, the seeking and finding, the hardship and bliss.

The vague religiosity of our current society is fixated almost entirely on the individual. It is all about personal experiences, self-discovery, unconditional self-acceptance, self-caressing, becoming one with oneself, awakening innermost potentials, finding the divine in oneself, and ultimately reinventing oneself. (Regrettably, even a few Christian theologians are riding this wave today.)

This, however, does not correspond with the essence of biblical faith. The Bible essentially recounts that God has a people in the world, from whom one can learn what God wants for and with all nations. Of course, the individual matters in all this. Personal callings, freedom, and responsibility are all things no one can assume for anyone else. Yet an individual's personal standing is impossible without the cooperation of the many, helping and standing in for one another. God needs a people in the world to show, intelligibly, how freedom and human dignity can be found.

This is exactly what the great story of Israel's liberating exodus out of Egypt tells us (Exod 12—15). In this, we can take Egypt to stand for the prototypical "theocracy." What does *theocracy* mean? It stands for the complete and inseparable union between religion, society, culture, and state. The Egyptian pharaoh was considered godlike. He and his civil servants were the guarantors of the country's fortunes and well-being. The state intervened and had a hand in all social relations. Today, we would call this a totalitarian state, or the seamless fusion of state and religion. There was no freedom in biblical Egypt but a vast number of slaves and migrant workers who worked for the state on huge construction sites (Exod 1:11; 5:6–9).

Abraham's descendants end up in this highly organized theocracy because a famine had ravaged their homeland and put them in dire need. They fled to

Egypt, where they became an important group whom the Egyptians came to fear (Exod 1:1–14). At this point the Bible recalls what happened to Israel in Egypt. They didn't *adapt* to the theocratic structure of Egyptian society, nor did they *revolt* against it. Instead, they *departed* from it in what we know as the *exodus*. God's great plan and the fusion of state and religion simply did not match up. Israel's flight from Egypt pursued an altogether different objective, something totally new. It was to become a people that was not a state but wholly focused and directed at God and to become a people gathered out of free consent. This, however, was unheard of in the world of the ancient Middle East.

The exodus story becomes the foundation for everything else the People of God experience in their history, and it is equally fundamental for the Church. To this day, the Church therefore celebrates its exodus from Egypt during the Easter Vigil* as a recollection of its own liberation from the old world with its enslavements, the liberating rescue from its own bondage into a new life given by God.

Leaving the tried and tested behind is always risky, anything but harmless, and does not come cheap. It is a risk that the people of God will need to repeat time and again. It began with Abraham, continued with Moses and the prophets, and culminated in Jesus. Anyone who becomes a Christian takes part in this incredible history, dares to count on the enterprise of faith, and becomes a link in the chain of the people of God that runs through the centuries. It is a three-thousand-year-old history that one steps into. When I pray the Magnificat*, it sometimes sends a chill down my spine as I speak with Mary, mother of God:

> He has brought down the powerful from their thrones,
> and lifted up the lowly;

Exodus Out of Egypt

he has filled the hungry with good things,
 and sent the rich away empty.
He has helped his servant Israel,
 in remembrance of his mercy,
according to the promise he made to our ancestors,
 to Abraham and to his descendants forever.
  (Luke 1:52–55)

This New Testament canticle recalls the memory of God's mighty deeds in the history of the people of God.

> I greet you both with all my heart and
> a special hello to Anna.

Letter 12

DEATH IN THE SEA OF REEDS

Dear Beth,

Our exchange is really turning into a thrilling conversation. You told me that what I had written about Israel's liberation from Egypt was new to both of you, so you went and bought yourself a Bible to read the exodus story. You reacted with horror and wrote, "God himself destroys thousands of lives at the Sea of Reeds, and afterward this drowning orgy is rapturously celebrated."

Your husband continued reading, finding massacre upon massacre, all committed in the name of God or by God himself. "Is this the new freedom and human dignity you praise?" you ask, adding, "How are we ever to explain this to Anna? We are not capable of it…and actually don't want to."

Dear Beth, it is good that both of you should raise this question of violence in the Bible so early. It is one that must—and can—be clarified. This very question reveals that the Bible is not a personal and literal dictate coming out of God's mouth but has a different origin and history. In stark contrast to what Islam claims regarding the Qur'an, the Bible is "God's word *in human words*," that is, it is indeed the word of the living God, but the word as received, understood, and formulated by human beings over an extended history until it found its unequivocal reception in Jesus, who is God's revealed and final word.

Before I address the destruction of Pharaoh's army in the Sea of Reeds, I would, however, like to add a word regarding Anna!

You are right in your quest to protect your child against cruel brutalities. However, we must ensure that we do not confuse the real horrors of our society, which do real harm to the souls of children, with storylines in which the bad are conquered and the good are saved. For example, if media-addicted kids use their smartphones during school breaks to share clips of animals suffering wretched deaths, actual executions, or pornographic violence with their peers, we should be highly alarmed. Narratives, on the other hand, which keep a much greater distance simply by being "stories," and in which good wins in the end, are of a totally different kind. These narrations do no harm to children, as they love them and even need them because children long for justice.

The exodus story describes Pharaoh as a highly obstinate, malicious ruler who enslaves a whole people without a second thought (Exod 1:11–14) and commands that all male children born to the Israelites be drowned in the Nile (Exod 1:15–22). This is the very fate that is then meted out to the Egyptian army as they perish in the waters of the sea.

The story's intent is to say that contempt for humanity always comes back to take revenge on earth. Above all, though, it wants to show clearly that God rescues from peril those who entrust themselves to God. More still, the exodus narrative wants to demonstrate that this people, chosen by God out of love, is so important to God and that he will not let them perish. God needs them to change the world. If you can show Anna that these messages are conveyed in the story, you need not worry about her.

Allow me to add one more principal aspect on the violence in the Old Testament: Yes, it exists, and sometimes it even starts with God! If we stumble on the respective biblical passages, we need to be clear about two things:

First, many of these texts mean to say nothing other than that God cannot bear injustice. God cannot stand by as the innocent are murdered and the impoverished exploited. Justice must be established. God must restore the damaged rule of law. This act is expressed in the language and terminology *of the time*. Please do not forget that these texts are over 2,500 years old on average and use different tropes and literary genres than we use today.

Second, we must realize that Israel, as the people of God, gained its insights into God slowly and gradually. To comprehend and grasp the one true God, Israel had to deconstruct step by step the concepts that neighboring religions held and extolled for their gods. This ever-deeper understanding is evident in the Old Testament, as it is full of texts that clearly show that the problems of society and nations are ultimately not solved by violence.

The Book of Leviticus tells the Israelites to love every member of the people of God as they love their own family, indeed, even including the foreigners who live in Israel (Lev 19:18, 34). The Book of Zechariah describes the much longed-for Messiah as a king of peace who enters Jerusalem, not in arms atop a warhorse, but defenselessly, on a donkey, the load-carrier of the poor (Zech 9:9–10). Finally, the Book of the prophet Isaiah calls the Israel that has been crushed and abducted into exile the suffering "servant of God" who would rather let his enemies grind him to dust than resort to counterviolence (Isa 52:13—53:12).

Though the Old Testament does not theologically uphold these culminative statements throughout as only about Jesus, through his preaching and life he brings them to their final clarity. Nonetheless, the commitment to nonviolence is already evident in the Old Testament and even here casts a bright light on God himself.

So tell me in your own words now: Is a faith that was imperfect and incomplete from the start but had to struggle and work its way to an ever-deeper understanding not a much more plausible and humane faith? Is it not a faith made more realistic and human than one where God, so to speak, delivers truth ready-made and sent by special delivery?

I wish for both of you, and of course also Anna, that you find you are taking many smaller and bigger steps on this route of discovery and ever-deeper insight.

Warmest wishes to you!

Letter 13

THE SOCIAL ORDER OF MOUNT SINAI

Dear Beth,

What happened to us is a bit like Murphy's Law. Just as we were discussing violence in the Old Testament, and I wrote to you that the clips of violence pupils show each other during school breaks are the real destructive influence on children and not Old Testament stories, your daughter comes up to you two days later imploring you to give her a smartphone for her birthday. "Everyone in my class has one," she tells you, adding that it is high time for her to have one too, as her old cellphone is an embarrassment.

While you did not give in to her request, you did not turn it down either. Instead of just telling her "No way!" you as her parents sat down with Anna and, as I gather from your letter, had a long talk with one another in which you tried to explain to her the reasons for this temporary refusal.

Now, I know little about educational issues, but I am under the impression that you handled this the right way. First, because you and your husband talked to Anna together. This way she could see that this matters to you

and that you both think the same way about it. Giving
her reasons was equally important, but the crucial thing
was that you told Anna one doesn't have to do the same as
everyone else all the time. It is OK to hold a different view.
I think all this is right.

This incident told me once more how hopelessly lost a
child can be if she or he has to stand up alone against what
all her or his peers are taking for granted. Anna should
really have friends who do (or don't do) the same as she.

These friends would need the mentality or even the
properly appreciated pride of a small group that lives in
the awareness that theirs is a different style of doing things,
theirs is a different opinion, one that goes against the flow.

I think that these experiences should help us to
appreciate the history of tiny Israel. Seen from outside,
it was a poor insignificant people surrounded by
superpowers. Israel believed in the one sole God amid
nations beholden to dynasties of gods. Israel did not
worship nature but the God who created heaven and earth.
It did not extol power and might but awe and fear of God.
It swam against the current of mainstream religion. Israel
could not and would not be like other nations.

It must have been incredibly tempting to join in with
the celebrations of the Canaanites' religious feasts and to
take up the rhythm of their lives. First Samuel shows how
often this longing welled up in Israel: "...so that we may
be like other nations" (1 Sam 8:20). At these times opposing
voices could be heard: "Such a thing is not done in Israel"
(2 Sam 13:12).

Let us now look at the great story in the Book of
Exodus, where Israel assembles at Mount Sinai—God's
mountain—to receive the law. In the structure of the
narration, God offers the people saved from Egypt a
"covenant" or, better, a "contract." He will be Israel's God,
leading it through history, and Israel shall be his people, a
people that lives differently from the heathen nations and

thus shall become a blessing for them. Just as many other stories in the Old Testament condense the experiences of centuries, so does this narration tell us that all of Israel, the men, the women, the young, and the old, freely consent and approve this covenant (Exod 24:7). The Torah*, the "instruction" so given to Israel, is a social order that corresponds to the contract with God.

Obviously, this social order developed over long stretches of time and did not fall from heaven. It is an attempt to orient all aspects of Israel's life toward God, from the earliest morning to late at night. Everything, the whole of life, is interwoven with God, from the choice of clothing, the right food, the construction of buildings, work and leisure, the celebration of feasts, the relationship between the sexes as well as young and old. Of course, much in the Torah stems from the mindset and life conditions of the times, which is why much of it seems strange, if not altogether impossible, to us today.

In all this, however, we should not fail to see that some fundamental tenets of the Torah are surprisingly modern. For example, giving one's life the right direction is not limited to matters of the soul, the innermost, the spirit and mind of a person, but equally concerns the body, living conditions, and circumstances, the entire environment around a person. It addresses the "life-world" of humans, where everything proceeds appropriately and does justice to creation. A person in Israel should be wholly with and for God and thereby free from all powers that could darken and chain life into bondage. This Torah, with its many instructions and prohibitions, culminates in the Ten Commandments.

Now, there's a lot to say about the Ten Commandments, their prehistory, their exact meaning, and their historical impact. I will have to limit myself to a few central aspects. First, though, let us look at the actual wording of the Ten Commandments (two sections I have abbreviated) as we find them in the Book of Deuteronomy:

[Prologue] I am the LORD your God, who brought you out of the land of Egypt, out of the house of slavery;

[First Commandment:] you shall have no other gods before me. You shall not make for yourself an idol, whether in the form of anything that is in heaven above, or that is on the earth beneath, or that is in the water under the earth. You shall not bow down to them or worship them. […]

[Second Commandment:] You shall not make wrongful use of the name of the LORD your God, for the LORD will not acquit anyone who misuses his name.

[Third Commandment:] Observe the sabbath day and keep it holy, as the LORD your God commanded you. Six days you shall labor and do all your work. But the seventh day is a sabbath to the LORD your God; you shall not do any work—you, or your son or your daughter, or your male or female slave, or your ox or your donkey, or any of your livestock, or the resident alien in your towns, so that your male and female slave may rest as well as you. […]

[Fourth Commandment:] Honor your father and your mother, as the LORD your God commanded you, so that your days may be long and that it may go well with you in the land that the LORD your God is giving you.

[Fifth Commandment:] You shall not murder.

[Sixth Commandment:] Neither shall you commit adultery.

[Seventh Commandment:] Neither shall you steal.

[Eighth Commandment:] Neither shall you bear false witness against your neighbor.

[Ninth Commandment:] Neither shall you covet your neighbor's wife.

[Tenth Commandment:] Neither shall you desire your neighbor's house, or field, or male or female slave, or ox, or donkey, or anything that belongs to your neighbor. (Deut 5:6–21)

As I wrote before, I can highlight only the most significant aspects here. Preceding the Ten Commandments is a short prologue: "I am the LORD your God, who brought you out of the land of Egypt, out of the house of slavery," which makes clear that the Ten Commandments are not free-floating commands from God and certainly not a load to burden human beings.

Instead, they are a "reaction" to what God has already done for his people. God has led them into freedom, so that observing these instructions is the grateful answer to God's deeds. Naturally, this also applies today, because God acts on us in baptism, leads us into a new land of the fellowship of the Church, where God grants us freedom. For those who entrust themselves to God and adhere to his commandments are free from countless coercions. They avoid the chaos into which we are ultimately driven by the many "liberties" we allow ourselves.

What's more, all the commandments are preceded by the commitment to worship the *one* God alone. Israel must not serve any foreign gods or their images, which sought to make the Divine present and real. In this central aspect Israel set itself apart from all other religions, as the surrounding people had countless imposing gods that would meticulously reflect very human desires. Yet Israel was prohibited from serving them, even if such service was extremely tempting. This commandment is equally binding for Christians because we keep creating our own gods, whom we not only serve but with whom we are often besotted. Power over others, the nation, money, rampant luxury, unchecked greed, an egomania that knows nothing but itself: all of this can become a god lording it over us, the highest and ultimate, to whom we give ourselves.

One chapter later, in the Book of Deuteronomy, the First Commandment is taken up again and outlined with more precision and depth. So we read in 6:4–5, "Hear, O Israel: The LORD is our God, the LORD alone. You shall love the LORD your God with all your heart, and with all your soul, and with all your might."

This means that God cannot be a side issue and that we should certainly refrain from misusing God for our own interests. All we can do is to "love" God, that is, to give oneself over to God freely and with one's whole existence.

There is so much more to say about the Ten Commandments and the Torah. But my letter would become too long, so suffice it to say this one thing: I am often pained in my soul when many of our contemporaries take pride in the Age of Enlightenment without the faintest idea of where most of their liberties and historical achievements take their root. The day off in the rhythm of the week, our big festive seasons, the respect for property, and the right to dignity of the individual, the right to privacy, and even against third-party access to our home, all this and much more we owe to the Old Testament.

Kindest regards to all of you today.

Letter 14

ANCHORING HUMAN RIGHTS

Dear Beth,

You expressed your gratitude for what I had to say about the Ten Commandments and that I listed them (almost) in their entirety. You had two questions you wanted to ask. First, you asked where in the Torah does one read about "protecting the home against third-party intrusion," which you felt was highly remarkable and had never heard of anywhere before.

Well, this question is easy to answer. The Book of Deuteronomy also covers the question of how a loan is to be settled. In the agrarian society of Israel, loans were used primarily in case a farmer had lost a whole year's harvest through pests or droughts. The rich had to step in by granting them credit without making any interest from the funds, however. The loan was repaid with money or had to be redeemed through work and services provided later. As security, the lender could demand (symbolic) collateral, or a "pledge," but was barred from entering the home of the pauper. The privacy of the poor debtor was to be protected. So the relevant law reads, "When you make your neighbor a loan of any kind, you shall not go into the house to take the pledge. You shall wait outside, while the person to whom you are making the loan brings the pledge out to you" (Deut 24:10–11).

Your second question, asked on behalf of your husband, is a harder nut to crack. He wants to know where human rights really originated: "from the Old Testament or somewhere else?" Both of you are probably aware that the Universal Declaration of Human Rights was adopted by the United Nations as late as 1948.

However, reflecting on and promulgating basic and inviolable human rights is much older. The Greek philosophers laid the cornerstone, and ancient Rome's legal theory played a key role. A first systematic codification of human rights goes back to the Persian emperor Cyrus the Great. The UN's Declaration of Human Rights has many roots. Regrettably, the key, if not decisive, role played by the Judeo-Christian tradition in this development is largely ignored.

Think of the French Revolution's famous triadic call for "liberty, equality, and fraternity." The exodus story was a key reference for the notion of "liberty" over centuries, demonstrating what freedom was. Equality is a constant theme in the Bible. At Sinai, for example, all of Israel without distinction affirms God's offered covenant. The same can be said of the early Christian communities where Jews, Greeks, slaves, free persons, men, and women, all gathered around the common table to celebrate the Eucharist (Gal 3:28). Finally, the terms *fraternity* and *solidarity* have their roots in the Book of Deuteronomy.

Regarding the concept of "human dignity," the Book of Genesis played a central role: "So God created humankind in his image, in the image of God he created them; male and female he created them" (Gen 1:27). Not only does this clearly state that men and women share the same dignity; it accords them a dignity that could not be higher: man and woman are created in the "image of God." The Church has referred to this text time and again.

I could name many more such cases but will limit myself to one example. I believe only very few people have ever reflected on how the image of female dignity has been instilled in souls through the gentle power conveyed by the beautiful medieval imageries of Mary.

There is another issue of importance to me. The world's history has witnessed plentiful humanitarian ideals, honorable deliberations, and even declarations of human dignity. Crucial, though, is the question of whether they were "rooted in life," where they were actively lived, backed up by institutions that ensured that they could be actively lived. Much of what we today regard as the great achievements of the Age of Enlightenment had been reality among the Jewish synagogue communities or in Christian congregations long before.

Democratic principles, for example, were practiced over the centuries in the religious orders* of Christianity long before the proclamation of enlightened democracy. Abbots* were often elected by everyone in the chapter*. Solidarity with the poor and sick also has its roots in the Judeo-Christian tradition. Institutional care of the needy and poor clearly goes back to the Jewish and Christian communities. Hospitals for the sick, homes for the infirm and helpless, and institutions for the release of prisoners are Christian inventions.

Human rights require places where they are lived proactively and where their justification is anchored in God, because otherwise they wilt and dissolve again. If the Christian faith evaporates more and more in its traditional host societies, it could happen that human rights, indeed freedom and democracy, could be called into question. It is no coincidence that firmly enshrined laws are twisted so cleverly and cunningly today that they conform to the current spirit of the age.

And it is no accident that we no longer speak of "God's Commandments" but of "values" and "rules." Likewise, "sin" and "guilt" have become "violations of rules." Values and rules are made by humans and follow the ever-changing ideas of society. Majorities can shift and change. God's commandments, on the other hand, are interconnected with the structure of creation and the God-given dignity of the human being. They are therefore inviolable.

Beth, I am deeply convinced that the hatred Hitler and his henchmen held for the Jews was ultimately due to Judaism's elemental observance of commandments that came from God and therefore could not be changed at will. Murderous despots cannot accept that "you shall serve God alone [and no *Führer*], nor shall you murder, nor steal, nor covet." This was ultimately the root of the Nazis' hatred of Israel.

I have struck a very somber tone here, but the state of the world is deadly serious. Free, basic, democratic rules and order are by no means self-evident. They are more akin to a shaky footbridge straddling a deep abyss. It is up to us to decide whether this footbridge is firmly anchored.

With such sober thoughts
I send warm greetings to you all.

REBELLION IN ISRAEL

Dear Paul,

Is it as sweltering by you as it is here? Here in the South
we have been experiencing near-tropical temperatures for
days now.

  Your last letter is also "hot," as you write, "It would
have been so pleasant if progress in the world, if the Age
of Enlightenment and humanitarianism, really followed
as smoothly and effortlessly from the Judeo-Christian
tradition as you describe." Your frustration is, of course,
understandable and correct because history cannot be
whittled down to the application of a few formulas when
one must allude to complex developments in a few pages.

  I am with you and think "it would have been so
pleasant!" The Church must remain steadfast in the long
and arduous path of becoming ever more aware of the
truth it is endowed with. It already carries the complete
field kit for this march but hasn't even unpacked most of
it. Unpacking it often involves the help of outside prophets
and external constraints. Though it has already realized
and lived other elements long ago, particularly in its
earliest days, it has all but forgotten them. However, the
Church continually keeps other elements alive through

its saints. Though "normal" believers may venerate these saintly figures and even pray for their intercession before God, they would still rather forgo the radicalism of the saints and of the Sermon on the Mount.

Why? Because the Church is not just a Church of saints but also of sinners. On its long trek through the deserts of time it has been accompanied by waverers and doubters, know-it-alls as well as the lame, blind, injured, and many almost crushed by their own burdens. Thus, this multitude makes only slow progress, with many stops in between and the perpetual threat of detours and dead ends.

The fact that the people of God still exists, despite all the guilt in its ranks, that the Church preserved the gospel and remains, despite all its wounds, a source of truth and blessing, is altogether an unfathomable miracle.

The Bible is all too aware of this miracle. Hardly had Israel been liberated from Egypt than the people complained and longed to return to the fleshpots of Egypt (Exod 16:3). As soon as Israel received the Torah at Mount Sinai, they danced around the golden calf shouting, "These are your gods, O Israel!" (Exod 32:1–6). The moment the messengers came back from surveying the promised land, they were met not with joy but with the spread of fear and panic (Num 13—14). Too often the people of God failed to believe in its God's promises.

The story recounted in the Old Testament over long stretches of history is a history of rebellion against God, of uprisings against his instructions, of complaints, despair, and indeed of falling away from God. Time and again prophets must stand up and show the people of God the right way by telling Israel, If there is no solidarity among you, no social justice, no help for the poor and needy, your worship of God is pointless and indeed all your sacrifices and praise will repulse God. "I hate, I despise your festivals," says the prophet Amos, "and I take no delight in your solemn assemblies" (Amos 5:21).

These stories of the people's rebellion against Moses and ultimately against God himself continue unabated in the New Testament. Many disciples abandon Jesus because they no longer believe in him (John 6:66). Peter denies him (Mark 14:66–72), and Judas delivers him into the hands of his enemies (Mark 14:10–11). In the earliest Christian community in Jerusalem, Greek-speaking Christians begrudge the Aramaic speakers (Acts 6:1), and later, they argue vehemently over whether the Gentiles joining the Church should be circumcised or not (Acts 15:5–7).

The Bible records all this in a rather unflattering way and without glossing it over. There is probably no society that recounts its own origins so frankly and truthfully. While most nations dress their origins up into heroic epics, in Israel they are mainly stories of faithless disbelief, disloyalty, sedition, and rebellion against God.

So I ask again: Why? I need to drill a little deeper here. The nations surrounding Israel were extremely pleased with their religions and did not quarrel with their gods. They built them countless temples, swore solemn oaths, consulted oracles, brought their gods traditional offerings, and lustfully celebrated their religious bacchanals.

On the other hand, Israel lived in a ceaseless struggle with its God. Why? Was Israel less religious than the other peoples? No! Even when Israel sinned, it still sought to be especially religious. But God wanted something totally different. *Religion* constantly seeks to place its own designs for life under the blessing of God or the gods. *Faith*, on the other hand, questions its own designs for life and asks only what the will of God might be.

As disconcerting as such intransigence on the part of the people of God may seem, it is nevertheless a sign that since Abraham's calling and Israel's liberation from Egypt, something incredible has happened in the world. A divine will is becoming visible in the world, and it is not merely another projection of human cares and desires. The history of Israel's intransigence is simultaneously a history of discovering the truth, and this reveals the splendor of the true God.

Naturally, Israel recounts not only its own guilt and infidelity but also its continually renewed repentance and conversion. It is at these points that the miracle of the people of God shines out. This miracle is not primarily made up of its achievements, the truth, the good, and the beautiful, which Israel brought into the world, but it is its constant *repentance and return* to the truth and its continually renewed probing and searching for God's *true* will. This is the actual miracle revealed. It is a miracle that comes from God.

Paul, we agree that "it could have been so pleasant!" Yet may we not add that the fact that God wants to make his people the "salt of the earth," despite their inertia and guilt, is rather fascinating? Whenever I read this word from the Sermon on the Mount (Matt 5:13) I think of a soup bowl. Without that grain of salt added to every bowl, the soup would taste bland and boring. Where Christians truly live their faith in the gospel, they are like the salt in the soup of what is all too often a bland society. I greet you all and wish that we may comprehend this miracle time and again.

PS: Dear Beth, I almost forgot to address the important issue of your brother. Because you see each other so seldom, you had so looked forward to his visit, only to be disappointed. When you told him about Anna's baptism, her first communion, and the path you have set out on, he reacted politely. But knowing him so well, you could not fail to notice the slight sarcasm indicated by the curl of his lips. As you write, "It was impossible to convey to him what moves my husband and me now. It's as if suddenly a glass barrier appeared, with my brother standing on the other side like a stranger."

The Christian Faith Explained in 50 Letters

Your experience has been shared by many before. Faith in God and following Jesus can separate us, can often tear things apart. Cracks often run right through the extended family, even through one's very own. Faith is a matter affecting all of existence, and it runs very deep.

It can alienate brothers and sisters, parents and their children, but it can also make strangers become like brothers and sisters. Stay connected in your heart to your brother Tom but keep confidently to the path that you have taken with your husband. As the prophet Micah says about Israel and the Gentile nations, "For all the peoples walk, each in the name of its god, but we will walk in the name of the LORD our God forever and ever" (Mic 4:5).

All the best!

Letter 16

JESUS, ENTIRELY OUT OF ISRAEL

Dear Beth,

Many thanks for your letter. Your brother's total lack of understanding keeps festering within you. It cannot be any other way and not just because he is your own brother! We all want to convey to others what we have experienced and what moves our heart. This lack of understanding by one's very own family is also to be found in the New Testament: Jesus faced the same. His "brothers," who were probably close relatives such as cousins, consider his public speaking and demeanor scandalous. They say, "He's gone crazy." They want to force him back home and under the control of the family (Mark 3:21, 31). In this situation Jesus distances himself from his relatives, and he calls those who listen to him and seek nothing but the will of God his brothers and sisters (Mark 3:31–35). Maybe you have read this very scene in the Gospel of Mark. It is easy to picture and tells us a lot about Jesus.

I also thank you for everything else you have written. The stories of Israel's rebellion and apostasy stirred your interest. So you read the story in Exodus 32 and vividly

imagined Israel breaking the covenant. You noted that
the story mentions a calf and not a bull, as I had claimed.
Rightly so, you demand clarification, and here's my
answer: It was a bull, as bulls symbolize dangerously
brimming and irresistible strength. For ancient Middle
Eastern god images, the bull was therefore highly suitable.
The storytellers in Exodus, however, refer to it as a calf to
highlight the foolishness and to ridicule the entire episode.
Anyone who turns away from the true God worships dull
"calves."

You showed yourself to be even more impressed
by the radicalism of the prophets. So you asked me to
refer you to a text you could read. They are plentiful. I
recommend that you read parts of the Book of Amos, such
as Amos 5:21–27; 6:4–7; 7:10–17; and 8:4–7. Likewise,
Hosea 11:1–11. Of course, it would be best to go through
one of the books of the prophets in its entirety. This,
however, would make sense only with an introduction and
a good commentary.

There is nothing like the prophets of Israel anywhere
else in the ancient Middle East. Their scathing criticism
whenever the people indulged in worshiping the gods of
neighboring nations is as outstanding as their courage and
self-sacrificing love when Israel had to be led back to its
God. Without Israel's prophets, Jesus would have been
inconceivable. They preceded him and paved the way for
him. Jesus took up and brought together what they had
said, perfectly consummating Israel's hard-won insights.
If I wanted to describe what Jesus brought together and
placed in final clarity, I would have to write an entire book
about Jesus. At this moment, though, I can merely give you
three key elements.

To begin with, take the first commandment, which
demands complete and perfect devotion to the *one* God.
God alone shall be Lord and not humanmade gods. For
Jesus, this Old Testament commandment constitutes the

center of his life: God alone is Lord. Yet, his Lordship is not static, hidden, and inaccessible. His reign is not confined to the heavens but wants to transform the earth, seeks to create truth, right, justice, and abundance.

God's kingdom does not rest but presses forward and is "coming." Jesus therefore proclaims the coming of the "reign of God," the arrival of the "kingdom of God." In Jesus's Aramaic mother tongue as well as in Hebrew, these terms are the same. The term *heavenly kingdom** means the same in the New Testament.

Jesus does not proclaim a distant reality beyond the clouds of heaven, but God's healing creation that presses on to reach its destiny, where God is all in all. This new creation will not come at some distant future time but today, here and now. It arrives in Jesus's proclamations and powerful deeds. It arrives in the person of Jesus.

Second, Jesus does not only radically place the first commandment at the center of his proclamations. He also takes the Old Testament word of Israel's election seriously. His message is not vaguely directed at all the world but goes out to Israel. He addresses the place where the process of recognizing the one true God had begun, where God gathered a people together in inconceivable love—not to favor it, but to call it out, so that it may be a blessing *for other nations*. God begins at a very specific and definitive place in the world, precisely because he cares so much about the whole world. Jesus profoundly understood and realized this "strategy" of God. The twelve disciples whom he sends out represent the process of regathering and renewing the twelve-tribe people*.

For Israel to fulfill its mission to the world, it first needs to repent. Justice, solidarity, forgiveness, and love must reign in its midst. Jesus brought together the commandment to love God (Deut 6:5) with the commandment to love one's neighbor (Lev 19:18, 34) and fused them into an inseparable union. The love of God proves itself in the love of one's neighbor. Whoever does not love his brothers and sisters in the people of God cannot claim to love God. Once again, Jesus is referring to the Torah as given at Mount Sinai and brings it to its culmination.

Allow me to add a third aspect, though many more could be mentioned. Jesus deeply internalized all the texts that, already in the Old Testament, establish nonviolence as a life principle for the people of God. Thus, Jesus prohibits his disciples from using any violence and allows himself to be killed rather than resort to violence. Once again, this shows Jesus as a groundbreaker for all times.

I must close now because I promised myself I wouldn't let my letters become too long anymore. I still hope that it has become clear that everything, really everything, that Jesus proclaimed and lived himself, comes out of the tradition of Israel, from the Torah and the prophets. Jesus sensed and felt the essential, pivotal, and key elements of this tradition in a unique way. He brought them together, elucidated them, and freed them from all remaining ambiguities.

He not only taught, though; he embodied this through his own existence. This way he became the fulfillment of Israel—Jesus is inconceivable without the Old Testament people of God. He comes wholly out of Israel and can only ever be understood from the perspective of the Old Testament. Jesus is an Israelite, a Jew of illuminating and unambiguous clarity, and thus "savior" of the world.

I greet you all with the sincere wish that you may come to love him as well.

Letter 17

JESUS, ENTIRELY FROM GOD

Dear Paul,

As your answer shows, you have considered and reflected intensively on my last letter. You write, "Yes, there have always been individuals like Jesus, people who brought developments to a logical conclusion and thereby effected their breakthrough. Charles Darwin was one of them, as he represents tremendous progress in biology. But Darwin also had predecessors, and his view on the origin of species was already in the air. It was *inevitable* that it would break through one day. Jesus must have been a person like that. He concluded what the Old Testament prophets had begun."

Allow me this long quotation from your letter to give me a clearer view of your thought. What you write is correct in a way, although in the history of faith nothing happens "inevitably." It may well be in the natural sciences that specific advances and insights *are bound* to come up at some point. Faith, however, relies on listening, free decision, and conversion. None of this is inevitable. Still, you are right when you say that Jesus concluded what the

Old Testament prophets had begun. He consummates, fulfills, and perfects.

If we want to get closer to Jesus, this is but *one* side. Though Jesus is the fruit of the faith's long history that began with Abraham, Jesus would be inconceivable without Israel's preceding growth in knowledge. This statement by itself does not suffice, though, because with Jesus, something comes into the world that cannot be deduced from Israel's history. The Gospel of Matthew tries to find words for this different and new quality by saying Jesus is "from the Holy Spirit" (Matt 1:20).

This formulation expresses exactly what this letter wants to show. Jesus is the fruit of Israel's history, while in his person he is so much more than this history. Jesus comes not only *entirely* out of Israel's history but also *entirely* out of God.

Much like Matthew, the Gospel of Luke phrases it in the sequence where the angel interprets the mystery of Jesus for Mary: "The Holy Spirit will come upon you, and the power of the Most High will overshadow you; therefore the child to be born will be holy; he will be called Son of God" (Luke 1:35). The Apostles' Creed* takes up this wording and formulates it thus: "Jesus Christ... conceived by the Holy Spirit, born of the Virgin Mary."

Let us not mistake these statements, that Jesus is "from the Holy Spirit" or even was "conceived by the Holy Spirit." They do not mean that in Jesus's conception the Holy Spirit assumed the *biological* role of the man. Nor do they mean to say that Jesus, like Greek heroes who had human mothers, apparently had a God as his *begetting* procreator and thus was a hybrid being, a "demi-god"— half god, half man. The Church never meant this and has indignantly rejected any such myths.

In an earlier letter, I alluded to the continuous dialog between God and creation, between God and humans. Let me take up this notion once more to get closer to Jesus from this angle. The dialog between God and humans is finally and fully perfected in Jesus. Jesus is the "Word" as such. He is God's definitive word to the world, a word that says everything, that reveals everything. In Jesus, God has disclosed himself entirely. At the same time, Jesus is the full and final word that the world says to God. For in Mary, who said her yes as the representative of all of Israel, the word of God was received and taken in complete devotion and without any rebellion. And so, the Word of God could become flesh (John 1:14).

When God comes into the world himself, though, this transcends all possibilities of creation, of nature and history. We need to emphasize this other side with the same forcefulness as we stress Jesus's origin in Israel. Only in this way can we do justice to the mystery of his person.

This is also the way to understanding the title "Son of God," which the evangelist Luke brings into immediate connection with the Holy Spirit coming upon Mary. Obviously, Jesus is not God's son in the biological sense and is not "son" the way *we* speak of sons as our natural offspring. The term *son* here is used metaphorically, as always when we speak of God. Just as a child, son or daughter, has this inseparable closeness to its parents, so does Jesus have an unfathomable bond to his heavenly Father. This is a mystery of the faith, and yet we must try to think and confess to this mystery using our own terms and concepts.

During its early centuries, the Church sought to comprehend and elaborate all the immediate experiences made by Jesus's disciples and recorded by them in the writings of the New Testament. The Council* of Chalcedon* in AD 451 marked the high point of these reflections as it sought to protect them from aberrations and heretical teachings. The council put it thus: Jesus is wholly human and wholly God, "united without mixing, blending, or alteration." Thus, Jesus is not half man and half God but both in full. He is a true man, and yet in him God has become fully present in our world.

This is neither totally inconceivable nor unthinkable for Israel's understanding of God. The Old Testament tells us that God "dwells" among his people, namely, in the Holy Tent during the desert wanderings and later in the Temple in Jerusalem (Exod 40:34–38; 1 Kgs 8:10–11). Accordingly, the author of the Letter to the Colossians notes that God "dwells" within Jesus (Col 1:19; 2:9). And the author of the Gospel of John formulates, "The Word became flesh and lived among us" (John 1:14).

This phenomenon of God's "dwelling" among his people shows that the Church does not deviate from the Old Testament. It does not dilute the faith of Israel with absurdities but instead takes the fundamental principles of the Old Testament utterly and radically seriously.

Paul, this has turned into a highly theological letter. Alas, this is what it is all about. We try to comprehend the mysteries of the Christian faith theologically, which means from the strength of the Christian tradition as well as the strength of human reason, though there is still much more to be said.

I greet both of you very warmly and wish you a
heart open to the miracle of the incarnation
and the power of the Holy Spirit.

Letter 18

JESUS, GOD'S PRESENCE IN THE WORLD

Dear Beth and Paul,

I had begun to get seriously worried as your letters had always come hard and fast so far. We were engaged in a real back-and-forth conversation. Then suddenly there was no email from you in my inbox for the last ten days. Did you both catch the summer flu? Or did meeting the brother(-in-law) reverberate much longer and stronger? Or was it the topic of my last letter?

Now your letter from yesterday showed me it was indeed the topic. You wrote, "We were simply somewhat taken aback. What you wrote about 'conceived by the Holy Spirit' and 'wholly human and wholly God' is not only hard to stomach but also terribly far from us. What are we to make of it? Whom does it help? Does it help against the need in this world?"

I will try to answer this in three steps. First, you surely remember that in my letters I keep returning to the creation and that God created the world out of love: a love that gives—what's more, a love that doesn't just give a gift, but a love that gives itself away. This fundamental move of God carries and fulfills creation right from the start. Jesus is the culmination of this, God's gift of himself to his creation.

In Jesus, God is giving himself. Jesus is God's complete presence in our world, and creation has reached its destination. By God becoming present in the human being Jesus, the world has become, at least in Jesus, fully that for which it was created. God is now entirely in the world. The infinitely distant God, who is so unfathomable and unspeakable to us, is now right in our midst. We can see him, look at him. God has become our flesh and blood.

That is something of incredible beauty; the earth is no longer just a heap of dirt and misery, but more than a lost dust particle floating around the cosmos. History is no theater of the absurd but has become valuable and good in Jesus, loved by God, and accepted in all eternity. Jesus is the place and guarantor of God's perfect presence. Is this so distant from us? Is it of no significance? Is it not deeply consoling?

Second, we had already spoken at length about creation and history not unfolding as they could have. God wanted a *free* world and *free* human beings, which, however, entailed the possibility of standstill, negation, and refusal. These possibilities have sadly turned into reality. We live in a history marked, not just by much goodness, but equally by aberrations, meanness, and terror.

The potentials of evil, however, bring suffering, cause chaos and confusion, and create darkness and nameless misery. How is help to come into this confused and hopeless world? It will come if at least one place reveals, visible to all, what God wants, what God's plan is, and where salvation can be found. Jesus is this point and place, for God tells us in Jesus, in whom he himself became human, what God's will is, *how* he brings deliverance and *how* salvation becomes possible. God does not tell us with mere words, a pompous manifesto or a "party platform," but in Jesus.

This is how God saves and redeems. Not with nice words—God bestows *the* Word, bestows his Son on us, and hence also himself. Thus, he steps right into the squalor we have created, the chaos we have sown. God does this to liberate us.

Third, God does not do this with magic or sorcerer's tricks but by becoming *truly* human. Greco-Roman antiquity imagined that their gods could don a fake body to walk the earth for a short while, during which they "dress up" as humans.

The Christian faith says something utterly different. It professes that God became truly human in Jesus. Becoming truly human is impossible without a long history preparing for this event. It is impossible without a people willing to listen and change their ways time and again. And it is impossible without a mother, who says her unequivocal yes to this event, with her entire existence, body, soul, and mind, and who says so in the name of and on behalf of all of Israel. This is meant when we speak of Mary's "virginity," above everything else: that she says her yes not half-heartedly but with the absolute inimitability and undivided devotion to what is to happen to her. A "pure" heart is an undivided heart, which entrusts itself absolutely to God.

Her son, Jesus, also had to affirm this yes time and again. In Jesus, God found a human being who said this yes to God in all freedom and, as the Book of Deuteronomy formulates, "with all his heart, and with all his soul, and with all his might." This is why God could "dwell" in Jesus (Col 2:9).

To recapitulate: salvation of the world is not effected by an optimum ideology, that is, not through the ultimate proclamation of human rights, a pitch-perfect political party platform (as necessary as they may be), moral upgrades of all and everyone, certainly not through a world police safeguarding law and order. Instead, the world's salvation occurred through God finally finding one human in the people God had created for himself, who, from the very first moment and through his mother, was absolutely and undividedly open to God. The world is saved through this person, who is the perfect "image of the invisible God" (Col 1:15).

I find this not only realistic but beautiful and comforting. So I wish for nothing more for you than that you understand this train of thought in faith.

Kindest greetings!

THE CLAIM OF JESUS

Dear Paul,

We are still trying to get closer to the mystery of Jesus. You said that you found this difficult, which is nothing to worry about as it is quite normal. Even during Jesus's own time, people tried to understand and make sense of him. Some said he was a great prophet (Luke 7:16); others considered him to be the reincarnated John the Baptist, who had come back to earth (Mark 8:28), while Jesus's enemies claimed he was possessed by the devil (Mark 3:22). Jesus was therefore already a source of controversy in his time and was even vehemently rejected. At the same time, many others saw in him the fulfillment of all of Israel's hopes and believed in him.

Let's therefore turn to your main concern, which your letter outlines in the description of the chat you had with one of your colleagues. Remarkably, this conversation was about Jesus (though rare, this does occasionally happen). As you write, this colleague of yours claimed rather aggressively that Jesus was a simple healer and wandering preacher, deified only later by the Christian Church. Your colleague referenced a book of a reputable and prestigious historian regarding this "deification" of Jesus.

As you write, "All of this irritated me quite a bit, because after all, it does happen that some people are elevated by their followers into superhuman figures. Honestly, I just did not know what to say to my colleague. So my question is this: How would you have replied to the assertion that the Church increasingly deified Jesus?

Paul, books that make such assertions are anything but rare and sadly are sometimes even penned by theologians. Usually they just regurgitate the old thesis that the Church posthumously deified the prophet and itinerant preacher Jesus using the terms and concepts of Greek philosophy.

Of course, everyone is free to decide what he or she does and does not believe in. However, a historian must remain objective in his or her description of developments in religious history. I'll give you an example from Rome's complex imperial cult.

Several Roman emperors were elevated to the pantheon of gods through a specific state protocol. While the departed emperor's corpse was cremated on a high scaffold, an eagle was released from his cage. The eagle's flight into the skies symbolized the deification of the deceased emperor. Witnesses swore on oath to his heavenly ascent, and the Senate ratified it during special proceedings. Thereafter, this emperor was declared a god and the entire process was termed *deification*.

When a historian uses this term for the Church's faith in Jesus, it places the early Church's faith in Christ on the same level as imperial Rome's god and state cult or Hellenistic rulers' divine veneration. Phenomena that are historically totally different are indiscriminately thrown together.

Historians who speak of Jesus's deification by the Church all too often willfully ignore that the belief in Jesus's divinity was not a relatively late development but was already evident in the New Testament.

The Claim of Jesus

The oldest letters of the New Testament already accord Jesus the name Kyrios, meaning "Lord." This is *the* very name the Greek versions of the Old Testament used for God himself. In the New Testament, this transfer of names is evident, for example, in Paul's letter to the community in Philippi (Phil 2:9–11; see also Rom 10:9 and 1 Cor 12:3). Moreover, Old Testament texts that refer to God as the Lord are applied to Jesus (e.g., 1 Cor 1:31 and 2:16; or 2 Cor 10:17). In the Gospel of John, Thomas addresses the Risen Jesus with this declaration: "My Lord and my God!" (John 20:28). The First Letter of John (5:20) calls Jesus the "true God and eternal life."

Whenever we read such assertions that the statements claiming Jesus as the true God were a phenomenon of much later periods, the relevant New Testament testimonies are diligently ignored. What's more, though, those who broker the concept of Jesus's deification withhold the notion that Jesus himself already had *indirectly* made this scandalous claim. The post-Easter profession is nothing but the endeavor to do justice to this claim of Jesus. I will try to outline Jesus's *indirect* claim in three steps.

First, Jesus *speaks* like someone who stands in God's stead, because he does not talk like a prophet, who merely passes on God's word. Nor does he speak like a precursor, who refers to someone greater who will come after him. Instead, Jesus speaks as one invested with absolute authority. This is demonstrated in the very frequent use of the sovereign "I" in the preaching of Jesus: "Again, you have heard that it was said to those of ancient times….But I say to you…" (Matt 5:33–34).

Second, Jesus *acts* like someone standing in God's stead. One example of this is that, according to the Book of Ezekiel, God himself will gather his people (Ezek 36:24). Jesus begins this regathering and renewal of Israel in the symbolic act of authoritatively appointing and sending out twelve men as representatives of the eschatological Israel (Mark 3:13–19). Another example: Among Jesus's enemies, those who are well acquainted with Scripture rightly ask, "Who can forgive sins but God alone?" (Mark 2:7). Now Jesus had promised people that their sins were forgiven (Mark 2:5; Luke 7:47) and consequently sat down to eat with known sinners afterward. This was a scandal for the Judaism of the time (Mark 2:13–17). So once again, Jesus acts as if he himself was standing in God's place.

Third, above all, we need to keep in mind that Jesus not only speaks and acts like one in God's stead. His actions are of *eschatological* magnitude, meaning they are *definitive*.

The position someone decides to take for or against him becomes a blessing or a judgment against that person: "I tell you, everyone who acknowledges me before others, the Son of Man also will acknowledge before the angels of God; but whoever denies me before others will be denied before the angels of God" (Luke 12:8–9).

One could list many more textual references here. Disputing whether all of them are from Jesus would be inequitable and biased. It was the experience of Jesus's disciples that God's definitive word is spoken in Jesus, and in Jesus, God acts definitively in the world. In Jesus, God discloses himself entirely, Jesus is the never-to-be-surpassed self-revelation of God. He is true image of God for all times.

It was this fundamental experience that Jesus's disciples sought to capture and verbalize right from the beginning by means of Jewish imagery and concepts. As the Church then subsequently further enhanced and reflected on these images and metaphors, it was completely appropriate and logical for the Church to conclude in its creed that Jesus is wholly God and wholly human. This professed creed does not deify Jesus belatedly, but just thinks through Jesus's claim that had already confronted and provoked its earliest witnesses.

Paul, do not allow yourself to be confused by catchphrases and slogans such as "the Church deified Jesus." Those who write this way have already decided against the claim of Jesus in keeping with "What cannot be, must not be," namely, that in order to deny that God becomes human, the New Testament testimonies of faith are downplayed with the assertion that the Church deified a charismatic, talented, wandering prophet. This, they assert, was born of disappointment over his death, and then all sorts of things were accredited to this man. The way the mere choice of terms—*deification*—is used for an underhand manipulation is wicked. This has nothing to do with scientific integrity.

So you see that when faith comes into play, things very quickly become concrete. We Christians are surrounded, not only by people who wish to ridicule our faith out of spite, but also by people who historically distort Jesus's claim.

Of course, no historian *must* believe in Jesus, and his disbelief may be founded on many reasons. He or she would then have to say, "The New Testament and the early Church saw in Jesus the son of God." That would be correct and would have to include the addition, "I myself cannot concur with that." Simply saying that "the Church deified Jesus," however, clearly oversteps the boundaries a historian needs to adhere to.

These kinds of transgressions are constant in our society, serving but to dress up one's own view of the world as science. Regrettably, radio and television programs are equally inundated by such selective reporting.

Sending both of you kindest greetings, I wish you the strength for critical discernment.

Letter 20

CAN ONE SINGLE PERSON REDEEM THE WORLD?

Dear Beth,

While we were busy in our efforts to understand Jesus properly, the reality of life caught up with us. Your daughter Anna had to cope with a major disappointment. While reading your recent letters, I had thought often of Anna. I was delighted to read she has become an altar server*, went to Sunday school every week, and was proud to assist in a service in front of the church for the first time. All of this brought back cherished memories of my own time as an altar server, which I owe a lot to.

But now you tell me that a few girls in her Sunday school class first ostracized Anna and then began ganging up on her. They were constantly talking behind her back and actively shutting her out. One of these girls told Anna that she would never become a real altar server as she did everything wrong. "At first, she did not tell us," you wrote, "and then I noticed something was wrong. She cried and

last Sunday declared she would no longer attend Church.
What are we to do?"

Under no circumstances should you just try to console
Anna and play down the whole matter. This issue must be
resolved! It is anything but harmless, especially since the
instigating girls roped in some boys, one of whom called
Anna a "stupid cow" and told her to "get lost."

Please sit down with Anna and have her tell you in
detail what happened. If the group of altar servers is led
by an experienced, trustworthy person, you should speak
to this person about the incidents. You will have to decide
yourself whether you want Anna to be there.

As a last resort, go and see the parish priest. After
all, it is one of his most important duties to ensure that his
parish* is reconciled and at peace. This should be followed
by an open talk with the altar servers who had participated
in the bullying. Often there are one or two ringleaders who
egg the others on. One should talk to all of them directly,
and if they don't take the matter to heart, their parents
should be brought in.

All this takes time and patience, but it is worth the
effort. Even in the worst case, if nothing comes of it,
Anna can see that adults are standing up for her and are
working for justice and reconciliation. This alone is an
extremely important experience for her. What's more, do
take seriously her refusal to go to Church. She is deeply
hurt and now associates her experience of Church with the
meanness that is normally meted out in schoolyards.

My advice is that the two of you continue to attend
Sunday Mass, even without your daughter. If you don't
want to leave Anna alone, just go at two different times. It
is good for your daughter to see that nothing should come
before Sunday service. But don't make a big issue of it.

It is very sad to see Anna experience this, and it shows
us something about our world. This world is crying out
for salvation. Initially, the theme I had wanted to write

about in this letter was how Jesus's death could redeem the world. Is it possible for one single person to redeem the world? In view of what has happened to Anna, I now want to turn to this question, and will start from the concept of representation.

Christian tradition says Jesus took on his suffering *on our behalf* and he died *on our behalf* to atone for our sins. Ever since the Age of Enlightenment, this very statement has drawn sharply divided opinions.

How can someone else do for me what I must do myself? How can I let myself be redeemed by someone else? Don't I have to make that effort myself? Don't I have to liberate myself? Plenty of modern ersatz religions aim at nothing but such self-redemption.

But does this do full justice to the real human situation? I am convinced, dear Beth, that the wish for self-redemption completely misses the point for humans and their reality. From the start to the very end of our lives we are dependent on others. Think of how we needed our parents when we were children! They fed us, clothed us, put us on the potty, wiped our noses, and tied our shoes, until we were able to do so for ourselves.

Next, we needed teachers, who patiently taught us reading, writing, and arithmetic. The fact that others helped us—introduced us to new ideas and fields, went before us with their skills and knowledge, and showed us solutions—wasn't that always the case? Even as adults we are always dependent on the skills and help of others. And when we've grown old, we will need others' care more than ever, need to converse with friends and acquaintances, need to rely on others' memories when ours begins to fail.

In other words, when I drive my car over a bridge, I trust the expertise of the structural engineer who constructed this bridge and in the diligence of the maintenance technicians who look after it. Every human being, indeed, every society, lives with the help of countless deputies, surrogates, and representatives. They can do things I myself cannot do and therefore help me with their knowledge. The Church in particular lives by the faith of its saints and above all by the path that Jesus took ahead of us all.

This representation is never intended to dispense us from our own deeds and actions, our own faith, and our own conversion to the right path. Such a representation wants to enable self-action. True representation does not incapacitate or disenfranchise us. Instead, it wants nothing more than that we become free to act ourselves.

This is the meaning of Jesus's proxy representation. He has finally reached the point that has always been the objective of creation: that humans shall behold and recognize God. Jesus recognized God wholly. Humans should be in harmony with the will of God. Jesus said that it was his "food" to do God's will (John 4:34). Humans should live in fearless communion with God, and Jesus himself established that communion. Jesus lived all this in complete freedom right until his death.

However, this had established for the first time an area of complete proximity to God in our world. It became an area now accessible to others, characterized by freedom, nonviolence, and love. I could never live all this out of my own strength if I were alone and reliant only on myself. I can, however, through the strength of what Jesus lived and what he gave the world forever through his death. And, together with many others, I can enter this area of freedom and reconciliation.

This is what is meant when we speak of Jesus's redeeming surrogate death. It is, however, a language that has become almost incomprehensible to today's listeners. It is not just Jesus's life but above all his death that is so pivotal, because his death finally revealed what his entire life had been from the beginning. It was total openness toward God, pure devotion to God, complete trust, absolute nonviolence, and it was purest "standing in for the others."

If I take all this and apply it to what Anna had to experience, I can see that she is in a situation that she cannot handle alone without outside help. True, she is also asked to do something. In fact, she had to take that vital step of asking you for your help. Now she must trust that she will be helped. Even more important, though, is that there are others who will support her: her parents, the leader of her Sunday school group, the priest. In other words, she needs people who want to help because they want reconciliation and true togetherness.

The Church is no utopian paradise, but a place in the world where we grapple with the truth, where we forgive one another time and again, reconcile with another, and seek peace among each other. Given the way human beings have become over the course of history, this is impossible. We cannot effect it or bring it about. We cannot do this without Jesus, who was the first to go down that path of absolute nonviolence and radical love and thereby also enabled us to take that path.

Beth, the way Anna is being helped now (may God prevent it from going wrong!) can reveal what redemption is: Jesus opened an area for us for freedom and the ability to turn around. When we enter this area, it grows in breadth because one day it will cover the entire world. This area began with Abraham and arrived for good with Jesus. The Church is nothing other than the lasting place of the reconciliation that Jesus bestowed.

Children who are barely nine years old are not themselves able to make something like peace and reconciliation. Adults, likewise, are not normally able to do so either. Peace must be endowed by role models, by saints, but ultimately a liberating and redeeming peace must be bestowed by Jesus and thus by God. Nonetheless, in Jesus's spirit we can all bring peace and reconciliation, and that's what matters now.

One of my relatives was a priest in a sprawling inner-city parish in a poor part of town. Occasionally I went to visit him, and his vicarage was always full of life. The bell kept ringing. People flocked in to speak to the parish priest. In the hallway he put up a poster that read in big letters:

> It's ridiculous:
> Everyone wants to change the world, and everyone
>   could,
> if we only started with ourselves.

As an adolescent, I thought this was awesome and really loved this text. I knew it by heart. It took me many more years to realize there was something amiss in it. Why? We cannot change the world. Even if we start with ourselves, we cannot change it. We only create ever more misery. We need to start with Jesus, or, better, we need to let him start. Only if we entrust ourselves in faith to him and the history behind him can we change the world with and through him. We cannot do anything out of ourselves.

In prayer for Anna,
I greet you with all my heart.

Letter 21

JESUS'S DEATH— A SACRIFICIAL DEATH?

Dear Beth,

Your letter was delayed for obvious reasons as you wanted to see how Anna was doing. I am glad to hear that your parish priest immediately agreed to the meeting and then managed to speak so wisely with Anna, the two boys, and the three girls who had set the whole thing going. I was especially very relieved to read that for Anna the whole affair has started to calm down. That she does not want to return to Church yet is understandable. Just let it work in her!

You also write that the whole experience had shaken both of you. Indeed, it always is and will be so if this happens to one's child or someone very dear. You yourself suffer with them or even for them. Allow me therefore to say something about the complex of the *sacrifice* in this context.

This word plays a key role in the Catholic Church and you will certainly have heard it before. In this context we keep hearing of Jesus's life sacrifice, his sacrificial death, the sacrifice on the cross, the sacrifice of the Mass, Jesus's sacrifice on behalf of the entire world, or the sacrifices we are supposed to make.

At the same time there is resistance against this word *sacrifice*, even in the Church to this day. Many are simply exhausted by the overuse of the word as in war sacrifice, sacrifices of catastrophe, climate change sacrifice. Who is sacrificed and to whom? Above all, we are tired of the pompous talk so loudly shouted during the first half of the last century invoking honorable sacrifice of life for one's country. Likewise, we are tired of hearing the all-too-quick appeals to the personal sacrifices we should make.

There are theological reasons to abstain from such invocations, as the old religions are awash with sacrifices and ritualistic sacrificial acts. The gods were lavished with the slaughter of uncounted heaps of sheep, goats, and oxen. No festive banquet could be held without a ritualistic sacrifice to the gods, and no glass of wine was poured without first sprinkling some on the ground in veneration of the gods. But from its beginning, the Christian faith drew a clear line to distinguish itself from pagan sacrificial practices, so why are we to associate Jesus's death with such a historically burdened word as *sacrifice*?

The whole undertaking gets even more questionable when it says that the biblical God had wanted a sacrifice for his gratification and reconciliation. Could it really be that God's unremitting justice demanded a sacrifice, even that of his own son? This idea seems to be lurking behind quite a few apparently pious texts. But are they backed up by the Bible? Certainly not, because the idea that an offended God needed a sacrifice for his appeasement is not a Christian idea. Instead, it distorts the biblical message, contorting and poisoning the notion of God. For it was not God who wanted Jesus to die. It was humans who wanted this.

A God who willed the death of Jesus must appear to any thinking person like a monster. We need to break away from any such ideas. I will therefore ask quite simply, How did Jesus himself appear? What did he start his preaching with? What was at the center of his proclamation? Was his public message in Galilee, "I have come into the world to suffer and thereby make up for the sins of the world. Follow me and suffer with me"? Or did his message revolve around the claim, "I have come into the world because God wants me to become a sacrifice for the redemption of the world"? Or did he propagate that "Death on the cross is the ultimate goal of my life"? If any of these were the case, it would have been tantamount to masochism, a glorification of suffering and a cultic veneration of death.

The answer can only be no; this is not how Jesus appeared. From the very beginning, his proclamation was referred to as "gospel," the good news. The evangelist Mark opens his Gospel with a summary of Jesus's message: "The time is fulfilled, and the kingdom of God has come near; repent, and believe in the good news" (Mark 1:15).

And when John the Baptist has messengers sent from his prison cell to Jesus to ask him, "Are you the one who is to come, or are we to wait for another?" (Matt 11:3), Jesus answers, "The blind receive their sight, the lame walk, the lepers are cleansed, the deaf hear, the dead are raised, and the poor have good news brought to them" (Matt 11:5).

The blind, the lame, the lepers, the deaf, and the dead stand for the suffering and misery in the world. Jesus goes against this misery, as suffering and affliction do not correspond to what creation should be. Jesus wants God to be Lord in the world and for creation to become what it was meant to be. This is what drives his message and his deeds.

How does this become possible? It is possible because Jesus has absolute trust in his heavenly Father, and he knows from this deep trust that God acts tirelessly, wanting nothing else but the happiness, salvation, and liberation of the world. Such is the meaning of creation. So Jesus must have understood very profoundly that God already grants his entire salvation *today*. All that humans need to do is to let it happen. Whenever we open ourselves to the will of God, the impossible becomes possible and the world starts to transform itself. In all this, though, such world transformation does not start with us, nor does it happen magically.

It comes about through Jesus's devotion to Israel, through his living with his whole existence *for* the People of God. This "for" manifests itself in many ways but above all through Jesus gathering disciples around himself. From him they learn trust, reconciliation, to care for one another, and to look at the people of God and not only at oneself. The disciples are to make God's care for the world their own concern.

Now let's imagine that Jesus's followers have become ever more numerous and have gathered more and more people around them, all of whom are fully dedicated. Then, let's imagine that Israel became known in more and more places, where God truly was the Lord, places where the prayers "Hear, Israel" and "Our Father" had turned into a lived reality, and Israel had transformed itself, and peace and reconciliation would have set in. Then, Jesus would not have died on the cross, and Israel would have become the shining city on the hill.

Sadly though, things turned out differently. The world ran on a different course. As we have noted earlier, humans have the freedom to reject and refuse, and the world can be suffused by the potential for evil that arises from these rejections and refusals. Jesus was attacked, slandered, declared an agitator by the high court in Jerusalem, and executed on the cross by the Roman occupying forces. Yet his dedication to the people of God, and thus his dedication for the downtrodden, the troubled and burdened, the despised and persecuted, did not die but is forever endowed upon the world. This is why we may and must speak of his life's sacrifice.

In the same vein we can say, as the author of the Letter to the Ephesians writes, "Therefore be imitators of God, as beloved children, and live in love, as Christ loved us and gave himself up for us, a fragrant offering and sacrifice to God" (Eph 5:1–2). These statements must not be distorted and twisted to suggest God had demanded Jesus's blood in order for reconciliation to happen.

God does not demand the blood of another but instead gives himself in Jesus. It is only in this sense that we can speak of the "sacrifice on the cross."

Let me return once more to our inner aversion to the concept of sacrifice. But those who have this aversion, though understandable, need to consider that no human being can live without the "sacrifice" of others. Put simply: How much time and energy have others invested in me, so that I can live as a semi-reasonable human being? How much patience, care, love and affection, time, and effort have my parents given me? Was that without any sacrifice?

Today's parents in particular experience, not only the profound happiness that children bring, but also time and again the sense of being overwhelmed by what raising children in the twenty-first century entails. For many, parenthood is an act of sheer will. They are drained and exhausted, lament the absence of time for themselves, the near incompatibility of work and family, the sheer survival mode of it all. The very fact that you cannot just send your child out to play in the streets of our big cities indicates the burdens faced by today's parents.

It never was much different in the past, though. In the old days, bitter poverty and rampant disease took many infant lives and caused parents deep pain. Bringing children into this world was always associated with sacrifice as well as with joy. We all live because our parents did not shirk this sacrifice. The wish for a life free from sacrifice is blind to reality.

Another example of this is the love between husband and wife. Even if we imagine a generally smooth partnership, it still requires sacrifices made in the daily dealings with one another, does it not? Anything else is entirely improbable.

No partner has the right to mold the other one into a shape of his own liking. In his encyclical* *Spe salvi* of November 30, 2007, Pope Benedict XVI wrote, "In the end, even the 'yes' to love is a source of suffering, because love always requires expropriations of my 'I', in which I allow myself to be pruned and wounded. Love simply cannot exist without this painful renunciation of myself, for otherwise it becomes pure selfishness and thereby ceases to be love" (no. 38). When we speak of Jesus Christ's sacrifice on the cross, it means nothing else than that, with his ultimate devotion, he was wanting to be there not for himself but for God and for human beings. This very deed, though, transformed the world, right down to its foundations.

Dear Beth and Paul! I am saying all this to you, the parents, having in mind the suffering you had these last few weeks with your daughter. Harm and suffering were inflicted on her and therefore also on you. This kind of suffering, though, keeps recurring in our lives. The question is what we do with it. Sometimes we can clear it away, but not always, so that sometimes we must bear and suffer it. If we bear it and bring it before God, it's possible it will transform itself. That is exactly what happened with Jesus, and many who believe in him can speak of similar experiences.

Kindest greetings!

Letter 22

JESUS'S RESURRECTION FROM THE DEAD

Dear Paul,

Many thanks for your last letter! Your objection shows that you are really thinking through what we are discussing. As you write: "Why these long explanations on Jesus's death, which all are geared to say that this death was something very special, profound, and mysterious? Why is such an infinity of mystery projected into this death? Doesn't it still say, 'Jesus died for our sins'? For what reason does one have to die for the sins of others? If God really were the merciful, all-forgiving God, it surely should suffice to simply ask God for forgiveness. Then God forgives and our sins are taken away. Why, then, did Jesus have to die for *my* sins?"

Why, then, are things not simple? Is it just the theologians who keep making it all so tricky and complicated? Or is the world itself so much more complicated than it appears at first? Let's think this through. What really happens when someone commits a sin, carries guilt, or commits a crime? Is it simply a tainted spot on his soul, on his innermost, personal core, that needs to be removed? There may be some sort of guilt in him, but God forgives that guilt and, lo and behold, the "guilt has vanished" and all is good again.

No, things are different! Forgiveness, though necessary and grave, is not enough on its own! Because over and above all the guilt, the sin inside the affected person has destroyed something that needs to be healed. Moreover, a part of the *world around* that sinner has been disfigured.

There are people who have been disappointed and hurt, whose trust has been abused, and who have suffered. All of this is not simply erased by forgiveness. In other words: *every sin has consequences*. Every transgression leaves a mark in the world, every crime spoils a part of God's good creation. The fact that sin affects so much more than just our own soul is what makes it so terrible. Sin embeds itself in the world.

Today, we have a much clearer perspective on these matters than previous generations. We can see for ourselves how fast we can contaminate the ground water, pollute the oceans with plastic, clog cities' air with dust particles, contaminate farmlands, and cause the polar ice to melt. These fundamental experiences open the eyes of today's generations to the disastrous potential in the world, as they not only affect the air and water but also touch on much deeper dimensions. We also witness the destruction and damage done to our inner worlds, the build-up of hatred, the demolition of empathy, human wishes, and even of human thinking. In consequence of the countless individual sins, whole spheres of evil have arisen, and these cannot be simply undone by mere forgiveness.

Holy Scripture tells us with many metaphors and images that in his death, Jesus descended into the depths of this evil and through that very act transformed and healed it. Through the death of the one who was entirely free from sin and entirely holy, but who had experienced, and even taken upon himself, the consequences of human sin, a new, healed, and purified creation arose. This is a creation in which we can partake when we believe in him and follow him.

This, then, dear Paul, brings me to the topic of Jesus's resurrection, which is what this letter wants to address. The death and resurrection of Jesus are closely tied together, and it is impossible to separate the one from the other.

Jesus was never closer to his heavenly Father than in the moment of his final disempowerment. And even in his resurrection he always remains the one who was pierced to death. Jesus shows his disciples the marks the nails left in his hands and the wound in his side (John 20:24–29). However, these wounds are "transfigured," and as such "transfigured wounds" they show that the resurrected Jesus makes present his whole history, all his deeds and all his suffering, for all time. It is a history condensed, transformed, glorified, and lifted up into eternal life.

When we talk about Jesus's resurrection, we normally talk about the empty tomb and the appearances of the Risen Jesus. Endless debates address the sequences of the Easter* events. The questions center around whether it was really women who went to the tomb and found it empty, or is this story a pious legend? Did the Easter events take place in the Galilee or in Jerusalem, or maybe even at both locations? Did the Risen One really appear before his disciples, or were these hallucinations of his followers, as they tried to overcome the bitter disappointment of their master's execution? Many publications covering Jesus's resurrection are full of such deliberations.

I am not saying that such questioning is pointless. The Christian faith never considered reason an enemy,

and critical reasoning needs to examine and shed light
on all angles of Jesus's resurrection. I do wonder, though,
whether these debates can convey to nonbelievers or not-
yet-believers the mystery of Jesus's resurrection. Here I
have my doubts.

Anyone who does not believe in God and therefore
does not believe in the creation of the world will also
reject the notion of the resurrection from the dead. What
is meant by resurrection is totally alien to these people. At
best, they believe in a constant creation and dying as part
of nature's eternal cycle. They cling to the questionable
consolation that "something" of human existence will
remain, be that impulses, oscillations, or molecules seeking
new constellations.

What did I read the other day in one of those—excuse
me—idiotic, esoteric manifestos? "We will all turn into
stardust, a thought floating the universe, energy fields,
a grain of sand trailing the tail of a comet. Whatever
form it will take, we will live on." These kinds of mental
outpourings have absolutely nothing in common with the
Christian belief in resurrection.

On the contrary. Those who believe in God, in the
almighty God who created everything and whose creation
is ongoing because he constantly calls the world into
being out of nothingness, these believers have no problem
believing in the healing and fulfillment of creation, its
elevation to God, and its final liberation and salvation—in
other words, in its resurrection. For them, the world
cannot fall back into unsubstantial nothingness in the end.

Why, then, create the cosmos? Why have such an
incredible biological evolution, which began with some
blue algae and went all the way to human beings? So that
this very human being, his whole culture and everything
he has worked for and created, is simply annihilated in the
end? I for my part would deem such an assumption totally
irrational if not outright absurd. Either there is a God, and

then also a resurrection. Or there is no God, in which case, all talk about resurrection is pointless from the start and a useless waste of energy.

One moment please, before I jump the gun and discuss the resurrection of the dead *generally*. I need to start out by looking at Jesus's resurrection. What is its meaning? What is it actually?

First, by resurrecting Jesus from the dead, God shows that he is on the side of the crucified Jesus. Israel's highest religious authority, the Jerusalem Sanhedrin, convicted Jesus for seducing the people, judged him to be a false Messiah and a blasphemer of God. So the High Council handed Jesus over to the Romans as the presumptive "king." The Roman prefect Pontius Pilate then had him executed as a rebel and agitator against Roman sovereignty.

Jesus was left to hang on the cross, seemingly forsaken by God, so that even those pious Jews who had honored and venerated him before must have now considered him as one condemned by God (Deut 21:23).

When God now resurrects Jesus from the dead, God demonstrates that neither the Jewish religious authorities nor the Roman occupying forces were in the right, but Jesus was. The Easter events put Jesus in the right. It is not only the falsely accused and convicted one who is put in the right, but also his proclamation of the kingdom of God, his powerful deeds performed for the destitute and despairing, as well as his entire life and appearance. The resurrection of Jesus shows him to be the true Messiah of Israel, as the real "son," the real savior and redeemer of the world.

Second, in an earlier letter I had written that "the disciples experienced Jesus to be God's final presence in the world. Anyone who heard Jesus heard God, and whoever saw him saw God." The Church held on to this principal experience of the first witnesses in the article of faith: "Jesus is the true God and true human being." So, if it says about this Jesus that God the Father had him resurrected from the dead, this means then that Jesus's humanity, everything that makes him human, his life, his story, his suffering and dedication as well as his happiness and joys, all of this is uplifted to God and fulfilled in God.

This kind of event goes way beyond Jesus, because even the New Testament is convinced that Jesus is not to be taken as a solitary figure or an isolated individual. Instead, Jesus represents all of humanity. In him, it is revealed what it means to be human; Jesus is the "human being" as such. If that holds true, then the resurrection of Jesus bestows incredible dignity on human beings and the entire humanity.

With Jesus, the archetype of being human, the *human being is actually* elevated to God in the heavens and it becomes finally clear what Psalm 8 says with such terrific clarity: "When I look at your heavens, the work of your fingers, the moon and the stars that you have established; what are human beings that you are mindful of them, mortals that you care for them? Yet you have made them a little lower than God, and crowned them with glory and honor" (Ps 8:3–5).

Third, the entire New Testament is convinced that Jesus is "the first fruits of those who have died" (1 Cor 15:20), the "firstborn from the dead" (Col 1:18). These formulations mean to say that the resurrection of Jesus has initiated the general resurrection of the dead at the end of the world. Thus, the end of the world extends right into the midst of history, and Easter bears exceptional weight. The Easter Day of Jesus's resurrection affects us all because Easter Day ushers in the final transformation of the world. The cosmos has reached its goal in the resurrected Jesus; Jesus shows what is to happen to all those who believe. The Risen One is the already fulfilled, healed, and redeemed creation.

Surely you felt that I tried in this letter to say we must think of Jesus's resurrection from the perspective of creation. This has often helped me to believe more easily and more firmly in Jesus, his resurrection as well as the resurrection of all dead. If only I truly open my eyes, I can behold the glory of the world. I can see the sun and the stars, the day and the night, flowers and animals, and above all the joyful or sad faces of children. And then I say to myself, this cannot be made all in vain or for nothing. It must have a purpose and goal.

Nor can it be made simply for an eternal becoming and passing. It must fulfill itself in God, who has created and willed it all. Then I look anew at Jesus, and his resurrection from the dead becomes the beginning of a magnificent and indestructible Easter joy.

In this sense I greet you, your dear wife,
and as always also your good Anna.

Letter 23

THE APPEARANCES OF THE RISEN LORD

Dear Paul,

You expressed deep disagreement with me for simply leaving out the historical questions surrounding Jesus's resurrection. The Risen Lord's appearances especially caused you headaches, you noted. You are quite right in remarking that any visit to one of the many New Age trade fairs will bring you in touch with countless dubious if not outright ridiculous phenomena. One is flooded with ads for "contact with the beyond," "ultimate wish fulfillment," or "getting in touch with angels and deceased pets." At times one is suddenly confronted by a "new physical gadget that can make your own aura visible." There's a profusion of "masters of spirituality" and wise sages and, above all, an abundance of visitors eagerly sniffing out any such obscure promises.

You are therefore rightly skeptical with respect to such mass fraud. And does one not have to accord this same skepticism to Jesus's followers' claim that they had seen their master as the Risen One? As you point out, is not every human being deeply inclined to hanker after

111

surrogate dreams, especially if he had just seen all his hopes being dashed?

Allow me to point out one first striking difference. These New Age trade fairs are all about business, big business flowing with plenty of cash. Jesus's disciples, on the other hand, struck no business deal with their message that Jesus has risen. Rather, they were derided (Acts 17:32) and persecuted (Acts 8:1), and many died as martyrs (Acts 12:2).

I think that even more important, though, are the many messianic movements that sprang up in Israel during the first and second centuries after Christ, all of which originated around a charismatic figurehead. Each time the leader met with a violent death, the respective movement disappeared completely and ceased to exist. They vanished entirely. One example of this is the movement that grew up around Simon bar Kochba, the "Son of Stars," who pretended to be the Messiah. His movement left hardly any trace and is almost forgotten. The Church, on the other hand, lives on to this day.

Having ventured onto the historical level, one should also note that Jesus's appearances occurred at different places before very different people. In his First Letter to the Corinthians, Paul lists them in 15:5–8 as follows: to Peter, to the twelve disciples, to over five hundred brothers (presumably the Jerusalem community), to James, to all the apostles, and finally to Paul himself. The Risen Lord appeared in Jesus's native Galilee as well as in the capital of Jerusalem. Whether all those to whom he appeared stood in any connection with one another is not certain.

We should also note that the fervent persecutor of Christians, Saul, had a vision of Jesus on the road to Damascus, which he himself recounts (Gal 1:13–17; 1 Cor 15:8) and which turned him into Paul. In no way can one

speak of disappointments and dashed hopes regarding
Saul. After all, he was on his way to apprehend Jesus's
followers as far away as Syria (Acts 9:1–3). Were we to
explain Jesus's appearances in *purely* psychological terms,
we would need an entirely new explanation reference to
account for Paul.

However, *purely* psychological explanation patterns
are simply not an adequate way of accounting for the
Easter appearances. Thus, if I say it is impossible to
understand the world without God, and if I further
assume that God communicates himself to the world and
through the world (albeit without disturbing or breaking
the structures of his creation), then the appearances of the
Risen Lord are intelligibly saying that the immensity of the
Easter event is breaking through!

If, on the other hand, I do not believe in God and see
the world as an entity devoid of meaning and purpose,
I merely see mindless matter in it, guided mechanically
alone, and am therefore virtually coerced to reject Jesus's
Easter appearances. In this case I will also always find
sufficient psychological constructions at hand for my own
explanatory ends.

Paul, I am with you when you subject phenomena
such as the Easter appearances to critical questioning. All
I want to point out is that such follow-up questions are
always influenced by preconceptions. Almost unnoticed,
though, these preconceptions usually steer the entire
argument in a certain direction. I freely admit that
preconceptions also abound in the Christian faith and in
theology. For example, the premise that the human being is
more than just an amalgamation of molecules, more than a
neurologically controlled machine, that he is not just made
up of body, but also animated by soul and spirit. Above all,
that human life has a final meaning and that God alone can
be that final meaning.

It is by these preconceptions that I live and that everything I experience, see, and witness confirms to me time and again that they are right.

Kindest greetings from down South, where storm clouds have been gathering since the early morning and we are sweltering in almost unbearable heat.

Letter 24

JESUS'S PRESENCE IN THE HOLY SPIRIT

Dear Beth,

Your last letter indicates that you have little interest in the historic debates regarding Jesus's resurrection. Your husband, you write, can really "get his teeth into" these discussions, but you are much more interested in what faith looks like in practice, such as in prayer or what to do when the Sunday sermon really works you up. Then there are questions regarding Anna such as, "Do we have to do something Christian with her, such as read the Bible with her or pray together?" At the end of your letter, you write that "the wall that went up between me and my brother keeps bothering me throughout. I tried to talk over the phone with him about the Church, and he just replied that he had nothing to do with religions anymore."

Beth, I'll come back to say a few words about Anna and your brother Tom later, because your husband and your diverging interests are more important. I think that I can understand your perspective quite well, but you should also try to understand your husband. Faith really entails both: the penetrating *questions* that keep coming back again and again, as well as the right *deeds*, which are done steadfastly and in full trust in the way God wants to lead us. Letting yourself be guided by God is not stumbling around blindly in the dark. Instead, it means looking at everything, everyone, and every event that presses on us, with a quiet attentiveness and the quest to find out what they might mean.

The New Testament and Christian tradition speak of the Holy Spirit, which leads us in these very moments. It lets us see truth and shows us God's will. Above all, it helps us to face the people around us in the right way. I do admit, however, that using the word *Spirit* evokes something different in all of us.

While some think of the genie in the bottle, others think of ghosts and phantoms, while some have fantasies and follies spring to mind. Most will relate it to reason and intellect, many to spirituality. So before I come to speak about God's Spirit, or the Holy Spirit, allow me to reflect a little on the experiences each one of us has already made.

Almost all of us have sat on a jam-packed airplane and have felt distressed by the cramped conditions. It started long before take-off. Standing in a crowd in the aisle of the airplane had been stressful enough; having to wait to reach one's seat and store one's carry-on bag in the overhead bin wasn't making things better. At last you are belted in your seat, wedged in between someone to the left and someone to the right. It is a tight fit, which makes turning the newspaper pages nearly impossible because it is far too cramped. Chatting with either seat neighbor won't happen because they apparently don't want to talk. So you find yourself stuck close together with other people and at the same time far apart.

Alas, this is no exception. Much the same happens at the checkout lane of the supermarket, a fully booked cinema, the subway. Spatial closeness does not mean anything at first. You can be very near a person and still be worlds apart. There is absolutely no connection, and you would rather keep that neighbor at a greater distance from you.

But it can also be the other way around. Take two people in love with one another but separated for a time, maybe even thousands of kilometers away! No phone connection, no email will work because no technical device is functioning.

Yet, despite the distance, they know that they are close to each other, they think of each other, and they wonder what the other is doing right now. They long for each other, feel for one another, jot down what they want to tell the other once they're back together. They chat with one another in their minds. So this example shows that you can be far apart spatially and still be very close. Despite the geographical distance, your *mind* can be fully with your loved one.

We all know similar cases of physical proximity and simultaneously unbridgeable gaps, or spatial separation yet still immediate mental closeness! Now what fosters such closeness? What establishes such a deep connection that, though it cannot be measured physically and is not made up of any waves or vibrations, still feels so real that everyone can notice it? What bridges these distances? And are these not the very experiences that give us our sense of the human "spirit"?

Allow me to give another example. You wrote in one of your earlier letters that you work as an administrative assistant and have had similar positions in several companies. You will surely agree with me that there are workplaces one just wants to get away from because of all the swirling tensions, arguments, petty injustices, and deliberately started rumors. And then there are workplaces that stand out for their lack of such mean-spiritedness and that excel thanks to their positive spirit.

I think these experiences can help to give you a faint idea of what is meant when one speaks of the Holy Spirit.

This Spirit is the "go-between" that connects believers, that bridges distances. It makes us go up to one another, even though each one of us wants to head in a different direction. It enables us to be close to one another despite our vastly different personal histories. It lets us become one.

The Holy Spirit makes the Church the international people of God, makes Christian communities the "property" of Christ, because the Holy Spirit is the spirit of Jesus Christ. It leads us together into a unity, despite our vastly different natures that have so little in common. It continues Christ's work, because Christ speaks to us through the Spirit even today. It renews the face of the earth because it is also God's creative spirit that guides the world to its destiny.

Though the Spirit is invisible, we can identify it from the impact it makes. Paul calls this impact the "fruits of the Spirit." In his letter to the Galatians, Paul lists these fruits of the Spirit as "love, joy, peace, patience, kindness, generosity, faithfulness, gentleness, and self-control" (Gal 5:22–23).

Beth, I want to single out just one word from this list: *kindness*. I can practically hear your question already: Has kindness anything to do with the Holy Spirit? To which I reply: Of course! For this is not merely superficial jolliness that is all facade and eager to score high on social approval, which can be turned on and off with a smile.

What I mean is the kindness that springs forth from the depths of the heart, which desires the well-being of others even if I do not understand them. This kindness is caring and full of affection because the other person is also created by God and I can pass on to them some of God's kindness. What I mean is the kindness that can forgive, comfort, help when help is needed, find the time for the other, and take joy in the fact that the other human being exists. Such kindness comes from the Holy Spirit, and it is more than any general vague humanism.

It reflects the "goodness and loving kindness of God our Savior" (Titus 3:4).

The Introit on the day of Pentecost, the entrance verse for Mass, begins with the words, "The spirit of the Lord has filled the world." These words are taken from the Old Testament Book of Wisdom (1:7), where they are preceded by the words: "wisdom* is a kindly spirit" (1:6). So it is a kindly spirit that fills the world, and we can experience it through the kindness we show to one another. Anyone who looks at another person with kindness and wants only good for the other, thereby proves that the Holy Spirit exists, and that God's spirit transforms the face of the earth.

There is another element of vital importance regarding the Holy Spirit. The evangelist Luke tells us in the Acts of the Apostles, which he also authored, how the Holy Spirit came down onto Jesus's disciples on the day of Pentecost. He does so in very vivid terms (Acts 2:1–4) but precedes this section with another description. He notes that the young community had congregated repeatedly before to pray together. They had pleaded with God, waited in prayer, and remained steadfast in waiting and prayer until the Pentecost day finally broke (Acts 1:12–14).

Why was this so important to Luke? Why is the day of Pentecost preceded by nine days of prayer? Why do the Jerusalem community and all of us have to pray for the Holy Spirit? Why does he need to be supplicated? The answer is simple. Because God's Spirit is the highest form of freedom and can come only to those who long for it in freedom. This freedom of really longing for it and really opening to him, is achieved in prayer only.

Dictators may force their mean-spiritedness onto the masses by working with coercion, violence, suppression, force, and terror, for dictators also long for unanimity, but theirs is a false, almost perverted unanimity, achieved only through manipulation and suppression. The Holy Spirit, on the other hand, is pure love, and real love always wills and wants the beloved other's freedom. That is why the Holy Spirit comes quietly, gently, often in complete silence, longing for our love, and it comes only if the faithful receive it freely; for the Holy Spirit itself is absolute freedom and knows no force or coercion.

Beth, why don't you just try asking the Holy Spirit to come to you and fill your heart? Maybe you will sense and feel a little of the Spirit, or you might suddenly find real-life answers coming your way, answers to the very questions that occupy your mind.

For example, take the question of what you are to do with Anna's faith. Watch your daughter; try to find out what she needs, but do so very carefully. When you think Anna may be ready to share prayers with you, why don't you introduce grace at your dinner table, of course, always considering your family situation? There are many examples for such prayers, and some can be found in hymnals or songbooks, possibly even those at your church. The United States Conference of Catholic Bishops has also published *Catholic Household Blessing and Prayers*, which may be a useful resource for you.

A word also on your brother, because I am convinced he is a brother anyone would wish for. He is honest in what he feels and says, reliable and loyal when you need his help. He goes *his* way and is loved by God. What you and your husband have seen and experienced has not been given to him, which is why you and your husband are taking *your own* way. There is no need to defend yourself against your brother, nor do you have to try and convince him. Just stay true to the path of *your* calling. If you do so, you do so also on behalf of your brother. We just don't know what might come of it. So you can be all at peace and be happy.

Many greetings to you, your husband, and Anna.

Letter 25

THE MYSTERY OF THE TRIUNE GOD

Dear Paul,

I was a little apprehensive as I sat down to write this letter. In my previous letters I have written at length about God, the Creator, and in some letters, about Jesus Christ, while the last letter had the Holy Spirit as its subject. This begs the question of how Father, Son, and Spirit are connected. It is difficult to find the appropriate words for this, which was the reason for my hesitation.

I shall delve straight into the main contention, then. When we speak of God the Father, God the Son, and God the Holy Spirit, isn't there an obvious risk that these three will appear to be three gods? How is one plausibly to tell an orthodox Jew or pious Muslim that this isn't the case? So this letter shall address the question, What is the meaning of the Christian notion of the *one* God in *three* persons?

Our present situation requires more than ever that we seek to clarify this question, because Islam is currently spreading with a vigor no one would have deemed possible as little as a century ago. Islam is promoting outright missionary propaganda, above all in Africa, but also in Europe and the United States. One of the topics in this propaganda claims Christians no longer adhere to their own Holy Scripture but have fallen into polytheism* and thus into idolatry as they worship three gods.

This charge was a central element in Islam right from its beginnings. While Muhammad had started out to battle Arabic polytheism, he soon also fought the Christian belief in the triune God. The Qur'an says in the famous 112th surah* (from Pickthall's translation):

Say: He is Allah, the One!
Allah, the eternally Besought of all!
He begetteth not nor was begotten.
And there is none comparable unto him.

This was aimed to counter the Christian doctrine of the Trinity*. That God did not beget is an attack on the Christological* confession: "Begotten, not created." Surah 4:48 states unequivocally that polytheism of this kind is an unforgivable sin: "Lo! Allah forgiveth not that a partner should be ascribed unto him. He forgiveth (all) save that to whom he will. Whoso ascribeth partners to Allah, he hath indeed invented a tremendous sin."

This also was meant as an outright attack on Christians, as they are threatened with this claim: there is but one sin that Allah never forgives. All other sins he can, if he so wants, forgive in his mercy, but the sin of placing other gods beside the one God is the sin God cannot forgive.

Therefore, any Muslim who takes his own tradition seriously must believe that Christians worship false idols and God can never forgive them. Their fate is *dschahannam*, hell.

However, Christians do not worship three gods! Instead, they confess expressly to a faith in the *one* God, the

God of Abraham, Isaac, and Jacob. Worshiping the triune God does not mean that there are three gods.

It says, rather, that all honor, veneration, and praise is accorded to God the Father. Worshiping the triune God also says, though, that the Father can be recognized and glorified only through the Son and in the Holy Spirit. So the question to ask is this: How could the foundation of Israel, this bedrock of the most radical monotheistic faith, bring forth such a way of worshiping God?

It began with Israel's experience of the one God, who liberates his people out of Egypt, guides them through the desert, leads them, saves them, forgives them their sins, and is close to them. This is not an absent, dismissive, distant God, but a close and rescuing God who comes to the aid of his people. Israel already refers to this God as its "Father."

This fundamental experience of God's closeness, which Israel has always had with its God, reaches a new dimension in Jesus. In Jesus, God has taken his definite presence amid his people. Jesus's disciples could not formulate it otherwise but had to say, Jesus is God's definitive word. In Jesus, God has communicated all and everything there is to say. In Jesus, God also acted with the same finality. In short: Whoever has seen him has seen the Father (John 14:9). Because Jesus is wholly the image, the true reflection of the Father, we need to say that he is the "Son" (Matt 11:25–27). This, however, does not expressly mean that he is a "second" God but that Jesus is the definitive presence of the Father, namely, the eternal "Word" of the Father in the world. From there on, the people of God can no longer ignore him in their prayer. All prayers to the God of Israel from now on are "with him" and "in his name" (John 14:13–14).

Pentecost* then anchors this foundation still deeper through a third basic experience, namely, that Jesus is—superficially—no longer present. His disciples cannot see him anymore; no one can hear him anymore. Yet, he is not torn away from his disciples but is right in their midst (Matt 18:20). Jesus is among them when they assemble. He is closer to them than he ever was before. He is with them through his Spirit. This is the fundamental experience of Easter and Pentecost and the fundamental insight of the Church as such: Jesus is present in the Holy Spirit, and with Jesus, the Father himself is present.

When the Church ceases its undifferentiated talk of just God but refers to "Father," "Son," and "Spirit," it is not a construction developed after the fact, nor is it an ideology directed against Israel's monotheism*. After all, this would be historically utterly improbable as the experiences outlined above occurred right amid Israel, that is, within the bounds of the strictest monotheism imaginable.

The first to formulate the belief in the triune God were not Christians from among the Gentiles but Jewish Christians firmly rooted in Israel's faith. Paul is an exemplary case. Moreover, the theologians, who in the following centuries probed deeper into the mystery of the triune God, did so to safeguard it against misconceptions and were not infused with Greek philosophy. If that were the case, they would have had to speak of the "prime mover," who is the negation of every multiplicity. So their thinking was not driven by Hellenistic speculation about God but informed by the New Testament.

The faith in the Father, the Son, and the Holy Spirit is therefore based on historical experience, in which God revealed himself. The *one* God took presence in the world in a manner that brought all his previous presence manifestations to their goal and fulfillment. Therefore, the Son and the Spirit are not two new gods, but the one God's revelation and attentive turning to the world, in which he now is fully present in the face of the image and the power of the Spirit. This is in absolutely no way polytheistic but rather speaks of the unfathomable and overflowing love God has for the world.

The problems with the Christian doctrine of Trinity, which many Christians also have, is first and foremost the distant position from biblical salvation history. There is also a second reason that I shall address in what follows. Many fail to understand what a "three-personed" God means, for they have no knowledge of what the concept of "person" means in this context.

Paul, I shall expand on the following only because I am aware of how you in particular seek to think through and rationalize everything connected with the Christian faith. After all, you really challenged me with the Easter events, and I appreciate that. So here we go!

What is a person? In our naive, popular understanding, we understand every adult to be a mature, standalone, and self-contained reality with full agency over itself. This compact and clearly delineated existence is additionally in contact with other existences of the same kind, that is, with other persons. Imagining the three divine persons in this way, we obviously have three gods who, while they might be in relation to one another, each initially constitutes an independent, self-contained reality.

However, already imagining a *human being* as a person, the concept of a clearly delineated and delineable reality is only partly correct. Looking at the human being, the question already beckons as to whether its personhood really is such an autonomous, independent, and self-contained existing reality.

To put it very simply: What really makes us a mature person? (Obviously, we have been persons since the moment of our conception, but what turns us into *mature* persons?) How does the (biologically speaking) initial cluster of cells become the person whom we encounter many years later in the *adult*? What we are talking about is a development, and it is an extremely long and differentiated development. A lot must fall into place for it to happen. It is impossible to give a full account of all that occurs in this becoming-a-person. The infant needs to be fed and cared for; its parents need to smile at the child and above all, they need to talk to it. The child is forever expanding its field of vision, its repository of known faces so that it grows more and more into a closely knit web of relations, first with its parents and from there with an ever-increasing number of other people.

The linguistic skills it gradually acquires serve to communicate the world to the child. The affection shown by the parents nurtures the primal trust, which is the absolute fundamental prerequisite for truly becoming human. The child enters an ever-intensifying relationship with the world, absorbing more and more of it. You have been through all of that with Anna.

So, what is a person? Not just a self-contained, autonomous reality, but always also the sum of its relationships with other human beings and with the world. This becomes most visible in love, in the act of turning to another one, in entrusting oneself to another one, in giving oneself over to another one. So, every human person is both a selfhood and also, to a most extraordinary sense, a "relationship," which is substantially more intensive than we normally imagine. We usually think of ourselves as resting in ourselves. But that is not the case. In fact, we basically do not exist without the relationships that make us what we are.

To test this, we would have to delete from our life's history all the people we ever met and ever had any dealings with—our mother, father, spouse, siblings, friends, relatives, acquaintances, neighbors, teachers, every other person we ever met. Then we have to delete all the books we ever read, all the movies ever watched, all the media consumed, everything that gave us joy, all the conflicts we had, everything we have ever encountered in and from the world.

What is left of us? A torso, an empty shell, a skeleton? In fact, nothing remains, as we have also eliminated the parents who conceived us. Being a person then means essentially being in relationships. Without the web of relations in which we lived in the past and continue to live in, we would no longer be who we are; indeed, we would not be at all.

And now along comes theology to say of the triune God that the Father, the Son, and the Holy Spirit are pure relations. They are not self-contained realities but, to the extent that they are persons, nothing but relations.

The Father is pure self-revelation and self-giving to the Son. The Son is pure emanation from the Father and purest listening to him. The Spirit is pure flowing forth and receiving from the Father and from the Son. So together the one God is an absolute "We," unimaginable for us. Thus, the mystery of the triune God reveals to us that it is not being-with-oneself that is the ultimate and highest goal, but being-for-another and being-from-another is the end-all.

To elucidate this crucial difference in the concept of the Trinity's personhood still more, I would ask you, Paul, to take a closer and focused look at the human being. I myself, my I, my Self, *does* something. I stand, I sit, I walk around the room, I eat, I go to bed at night. It is "I" who does all that. Yet, I am not simply identical with what I do. I am not simply my standing; I am not simply the process of devouring food; nor am I just going-to-bed. There always remains a center of activity that does certain things or doesn't do them.

Theology now informs us that this difference does not exist with the three divine personalities. God the Father is not in the first place only God the Father, who then does something else as well: that is, God loves. No,

Holy Scripture informs us that "God *is* love" (1 John 4:8). That means love is not another secondary element added to God, but instead God is nothing else but the happening of pure love. Likewise, the Son is nothing else but pure listening, pure receiving, pure transmitting and forwarding what he hears from the Father. The Holy Spirit, in turn, is nothing else than the pure receiving and bond of love between the Father and the Son.

I think it has become clear that when we speak of God in three persons, the concept of person we use is totally different from the concept of personhood we apply to ourselves. We cannot positively imagine the personhood of the Father and the Son and the Holy Spirit, any more than we can positively say anything about God. We can only ever speak of God in images and metaphors, where the dissimilarity is infinitely greater than any similarity. Even if we speak of the "three" divine persons, we need to be clear that the figure *three* is only a dissimilar term. It is something utterly different from speaking of three trees, three houses, or three people.

Despite all this, we are permitted to pray to the Father, the Son, and the Holy Spirit. We may and must stand before them, face-to-face, and address them in prayer because they are persons much more intensive and glorious than we can ever imagine a person to be.

Obviously, any approach to such a mystery cannot be limited to just terminology. The only adequate form to get closer to this one God is praise. Praise for the triune God's will to take us into his fellowship for and in all eternity, and praise for God's will to give us a share in his eternal life, which is nothing else but love.

This has turned into another very long letter, Paul, but it could not be any other way. I owe it to you and your wife to address the subject of the triune God not just by flaunting a few clichés. Maybe I managed to show instead that any talk of us worshiping three gods is nothing but slander of the Christian faith, because Christian talk of the *one* God in *three* persons does not contradict logic but is the strictest consequence of the insight into what personhood really is. Every human person is built on "relations."

You, your wife, and Anna do not live unrelated side-by-side, but you live out of the love that bonds and connects you to one another. The divine persons, though, are pure relations, pure being-referenced-to-one-another, pure love for one another and the world. It is a wondrous mystery.

Kindest regards to all of you!

Letter 26

THE CHURCH YEAR

Dear Beth,

Slowly but surely, I have an entire folder filling up with printouts of letters, which I assume is much the same with you. This also indicates that we have spoken about a lot already. Abraham's calling, Israel's exodus from Egypt, the covenant at Mount Sinai, the rebellion of the people of God, the prophets, Jesus, his death and resurrection, the descending Holy Spirit, and the mystery of the triune God who reveals himself through history. All of these are essential for the Christian faith.

So, the actual basis for the Christian faith is the narration of a story that is backed up by real history, with the Christian faith as the entry point into this history. Anyone becoming a Christian does not primarily learn the contents of the faith, does not acquire knowledge from the catechism*, and does not primarily acquaint themselves with some articles of faith. True, all of this must exist, and as we are dealing with real history, it is necessary that we should use precise and clear terms and concepts when talking about this history and its progenitors. However, the Christian faith is more. Anyone who comes to the faith lets themselves be *drawn into* this history, which began with Abraham and which reached its fulfillment with Jesus.

But how are you drawn into this history? How do you reach it? The answer is *by celebrating it*. This may seem a strange answer at first, so I'll explain it in more detail. Imagine that you have been married to your husband for fifty years, and you want to celebrate that wonderful jubilee. How would you go about it? A nice meal would certainly need to be part of the celebration. Your daughter and relatives would be present, and a speech would also be expected. Above all, though, memories would flow freely. I imagine you might hear the following: "Do you remember when we first met, how shy you were?" "Remember how we all had to wait outside the registry office because of that hiccup with the wedding dress! We all had a good laugh over it!" "Do you remember when Anna was born? What a life-changing day!" "How proud you were of your first grandchild. You should have seen the look on your face...."

These kinds of recollections would not just be an addition, something nice to have somewhere on the periphery. These memories are essential for every real celebration. Our lives would be rootless if we could not share memories. It is hardly surprising that many people invest enormous amounts of money and time in pictures and videos to capture their own lives as well as those of their children and grandchildren.

All of this holds equally true for the history of God with Israel. Yet it is all much more fundamental because God's history with his people must be "recalled" and it must be "celebrated." This is where recollections reach their very own depths and become "memory," which means that they take what God did for his people out of the past and turn them into the living present. As Psalm 111 sings, "He has made his wonderful works to be remembered" (NKJV).

The Christian Faith Explained in 50 Letters

When the Christian community gathers for the Easter Vigil to "remember" Jesus's resurrection, it is not straining its memory to recall something long ago. Instead, the Risen Christ is in its midst, and the community joins him on his way from death to life.

The so-called Church Year is just such a "memory" in the same sense, because in the Church Year, the entire history of God with his people, and especially the history of Jesus Christ, is brought to life anew every year. The Church Year is a memory from start to finish that makes the past present and alive again and thereby grants us a perspective for the future.

The Church Year is not identical with the calendar year, as it does not start on January 1 but on the First Sunday of Advent. And the Church cannot indulge in the practice of neutralizing Christian feasts with terms such as Season's Greetings, Santa Claus, spring break, and the like.

Nor does the liturgical calendar have much to do with the social occasions the Christian feasts have become, such as Christmas* turning into a shopping spree.

The Christian Church Year, with its old high feasts, does not live from ideas, needs, or moral appeals. It lives from a history that actually happened, a history of salvation and liberation that also encompasses us. It celebrates Christmas as the birth of Jesus Christ, who is our Savior and Redeemer; Easter as the day of Christ's resurrection and for us the start of eternal Easter joy; and Pentecost as the day the Holy Spirit came to fill the followers of Jesus with courage and confidence.

The Church Year is not only made up of these high feasts of remembrance and calling to presence, but these high feasts have times grouped around them that prepare us. Christmas is preceded by Advent, which looks ahead to Jesus's birth and his second coming at the end of time. Easter is preceded by the forty days of Lent, a time of penance during which Christians prepare themselves

132

for the biggest and oldest feast in the Church's liturgical calendar. The Easter feast itself is not just celebrated on *one* single day but spans a festive Easterly period of fifty days that ends with Pentecost. Alongside these there are countless feast days of saints that run through the Church Year like a string of pearls. These too are not artificial constructions but a recollection of a reality. They recall the reality of holiness that was made present by the lives of holy women and men in the Church.

Having listed all these feasts, I still haven't covered the Church Year in its entirety, because while running through all these feast days and periods, the entire liturgical calendar is permeated by the weekly rhythm of Sundays. The origin of Sunday is in the Jewish Sabbath. And this Sabbath is one of the greatest blessings we owe to Israel, as it interrupts the grinding flow of life and work. The Sabbath recalls Israel's liberation from Egyptian servitude and seeks to keep a space free for Israel to remember whence it came and what it lives for.

For Christians, Sunday, the first day of the week, has taken the place of the Sabbath; according to biblical accounts, it was the day on which the women found the empty grave and the appearances of the Risen Lord began. Thus, Sunday is the "Day of the Lord," the day of his resurrection, and the day on which creation is fulfilled. Every Sunday, we Christians celebrate the fundamental feast of our faith. And though Sunday "replaces" the Jewish Sabbath, it still follows this ancient Jewish institution, as Sunday is equally an "interruption." It seeks to interrupt our poor habits, our constant forgetfulness, and our entanglements in guilt and sin. After *one* week at the latest, Sunday wants to take us out again from the banality of our lives.

Beth, it was such a joy to read in your last letter that Anna has rejoined you at Church services on Sundays. Obviously, there is still a lot in that celebration that is strange to her, and she can't really appreciate the significance of the Christian Sunday yet. But we all must grow into these things gradually, and they will reveal their magnitude to us step by step.

I am grateful too that you two stayed faithful in your attendance at Mass every Sunday, despite Anna's refusal to join and despite all the strange sensations the Sunday services still hold for you. Your faithfulness has opened a path for your daughter.

> In this deep gratitude I greet all of you
> with all my heart.

Letter 27

WHAT IS MEANT BY *CHURCH?*

Dear Paul,

I have now sent the two of you a letter about the Church
Year but none on the Church itself. You noted this lack
of logic and rightly asked for clearer structures. In my
defense, however, I submit that the Church's liturgical
year celebrates the deeds of the Father, the Son, and the
Holy Spirit. That was also the reason to have the "Church
Year" letter follow the letter on the triune God. I admit
my mistake, as I never provided any clarification on this
sequence. So, you are absolutely right, and I humbly
confess my fault and duly promise improvement.

Let's then get straight to it! Why is there a Church at
all? Would it not suffice for the good people in the world to
come together time and again and stand up for justice and
peace? Because, after all, they can be found everywhere:
the seekers, the willing, incorruptible, helpful, and decent
fellow human beings. All they would have to do is stand
together and join forces with all the many institutions
that were established, especially in the twentieth and
twenty-first centuries, from the United Nations to the

countless NGOs that canvass and work for environmental protection, provide social support, care for the persecuted and refugees, and help during epidemics, famines, and floods. Don't they offer the help our world needs? Is there still a need for the Church?

There are undoubtedly myriads of organizations rich in blessings and in their efforts to make the world a better place. It is equally clear that much has already changed for the better. To give but one example, think only of torture, which for centuries was a customary means of ascertaining facts in criminal proceedings. Today many countries have banned the use of torture for such ends. There are similar examples, more than enough.

So, is the world not slowly evolving into a better place? Is the enlightenment and liberation of humankind not on an unstoppable trajectory? Many have thought so and many still do.

The Bible, however, takes a far more sober view. Though it does count on the good in the world, it still factors in the staying power of evil. It speaks of "powers" and "forces" (Eph 1:21; 6:12) that oppose God and ceaselessly bestow captivity and misery. The Bible even speaks of evil's growing might. A look at the wars and outbursts of excessive violence during the twentieth century, which by no means have ceased, leaves you inclined to concede this to the Bible. Every thinking human being must admit not only that there is evil in the world but that there is even a history of evil that is terrifying and equipped with increasingly effective means. In one of my earlier letters, I had mentioned that the first chapters in the Bible portray this history of evil, which is a history of increasing violence, in very realistic and objective terms.

At the same time, I also referred to the counternarrative that God initiated. This began with Abraham and its tool is the people of God, which is to be a blessing for the world. Now we also noted that this very people of God again and again objected to its mandate, rejected it, rebelled against it, and resisted their calling. We have seen how even Jesus, God's definitive presence in the world, met with disbelief and resistance. Jesus wanted to gather the people of God and guide them so that they would do justice to their calling of being "salt of the earth" (Matt 5:13) and "light of the world" (Matt 5:14). In the end, Jesus was eliminated as he was crushed between the millstones of powers stronger than himself. But these powers could not eliminate what he had lived for. From his death, his resurrection, and the Holy Spirit he bequeathed, the Church came into being.

The Church is not a new institution established by Jesus, and it is certainly no new religion, bestowed and installed by Jesus. Instead, the Church is the people, which God has gathered in the world ever since the days of Abraham and which Jesus gathered anew, sanctified through his death, and then sent out into the world. The Church is God's tool for the salvation of the world, the instrument in God's counternarrative opposing the forces of evil and doom.

Now this may sound pretentious and even presumptuous, but the Church is not all of this out of its own strength. The Church is what it is only on the strength of Israel's history of enlightenment and out of Jesus's devotion, out of his gospel, out of his death *for the many*, and out of his resurrection. Out of itself the Church is nothing. Out of itself it is powerless. It can only ever be a sign and a blessing for the world if it fully lives out of the preaching of Jesus and his salvific death.

Maybe I can explain this if I try to put into words what the Church is *not*. The Church is not an association you join because you share the same interests and are looking for leisure-time activities in a religious setting. The Church is not an umbrella organization that represents and caters to all conceivable pious groups and groupings. The Church is certainly not an "invisible" entity to which all who trust in the gospel clandestinely belong. Finally, the Church is not the head office for the satisfaction of religious needs, whose job is to ensure that birth, adolescence, marriage, and death are all elevated on the strength of some uplifting rites of passage.

No, the Church is a real people, international, visible, clearly defined, gathered by God, and guided and led into freedom by Jesus. The Church is a sanctified people who, through the strength of the Holy Spirit, live together in such a way as to create solidarity with and for one another. It is a real people that congregates every Sunday to confess its sins, reflect on and recall its origins, praise God, and celebrate God for his deeds. By the way, I think it is perfectly legitimate to wonder whether the United Nations and all the NGOs, in their humanitarian efforts, are not perhaps based in and supported by a Judeo-Christian spirit far more than they realize themselves.

I don't know, Paul, how far and to what extent you can agree with all that I am laying out here before you. Both of you already have an inkling of what Church *should* be, because in your wife's last letter she confided to me a problem the two of you share every Sunday: you struggle with Mass attendance and are really doing it for the sake of your daughter. The problem comes to a head at the end of Mass as you leave the Church. You feel that you have not had a real heart-to-heart with others in your parish.

All I can do in this situation is to ask you for a little "staying power" as you tell yourself that what really matters is the gospel I am hearing every Sunday and the remembrance of Jesus's death and resurrection celebrated in every Mass.

Moreover, I am very certain that you will have some very different experiences with the Church. During my life, I have met the most interesting people in the Church.

What Is Meant by *Church*?

What's more, they were not only the most interesting but also the most helpful and consoling encounters in my life. Even more, through the Church I met Jesus and the many who intertwined their lives to follow him.

I therefore ask all three of you for patience and loyalty as I send you my heartfelt greetings.

Letter 28

THE POWER OF THE SACRAMENTS

Dear Paul,

My last letter tried to make a few basic points about the Church, what it is and what it isn't. Afterward I realized that I had omitted something important, because I should have quoted at least one of the seminal texts of the Second Vatican Council for you. In the second chapter of the Constitution* on the Church, the council notes,

> So it is that this Messianic People, although it does not actually include all men, and at times may look like a small flock, is nonetheless a lasting and sure seed of unity, hope and salvation for the whole human race. Established by Christ as a communion of life, charity and truth, it is also used by him as an instrument for the redemption of all, and is sent forth into the whole world as the light of the world and the salt of the earth. (no. 9)

In the opening to this important constitution, the assembled bishops state that the Church is "like a sacrament, that is, a sign and instrument both of a very

closely knit union with God and of the unity of the whole
human race." Thus, not only does the Catholic Church
have seven sacraments, but the Church itself is a kind of
"fundamental sacrament." Now what is a sacrament?
What is one to imagine it to be?

I'll start by referring you to the above quote about the
Church. It calls the Church a "sign" of union with God. If
we want to understand what a sacrament is, we must start
with this concept of a sign.

There are numerous kinds of signs in this world,
and in fact we are constantly surrounded by them. One
example is that, when driving a car, I constantly see signs.
The moment I turn the key but have forgotten to put on
my seatbelt, my car emits a warning sound that persistently
reminds me to buckle up. In winter, a few seconds into my
ride, another sound tells me that the outside temperature
has fallen below freezing and I should expect ice on the
road. These prompts and signs stay with me for the entire
duration of my trip.

And I am not even speaking of the countless traffic
signs that adorn every road. Nor have I mentioned the
thousands of acronyms and abbreviations that supposedly
make life easier, such as MOT, ESP, ABS, DVD, ATM,
IRS, FFDA, FCC, IT, ETA, SSN, CD, BIC, IBAN, and
LLC. Modern life is awash with signals, signs and symbols,
icons, pictograms, and abbreviations.

There are other signs we use in our lives as well that
are much more important and more humane than all these
abstract figures and signs that smart people have invented.

Imagine standing at a major international airport
with an influx of passengers from a long intercontinental
flight flocking through the arrival gates. There are others
awaiting them; some having spent hours in anticipation.
The flight was delayed but now finally I am surrounded by
tumultuous scenes of reunions. Right in front of me are a
man and a woman in a deep embrace, hugging each other

as firmly as if they are never going to let go of the other again. I can see tears, and between each new embrace they look at each other as if to assure themselves that the other one is there. There is no need to go into this any further.

These welcoming scenes, these embraces, also fall under the category of signs. But they are a different type of sign, unlike traffic signs or graphic symbols. These are *personal* signs, which take place between persons. And this gradually brings us closer to the sacraments, which as visible signs express something invisible.

What is visible is the embrace, the kiss, the intimacy whispered into the other's ear. So, what is invisible? It is the love between the two who embraced at the airport, the bond between two people, the sharing of two human beings. Yet this invisible element needs the visible element, as the invisible will and must express itself visibly. Likewise, the visible also needs the invisible, otherwise the embrace would be vacuous, soulless, and superficial.

We need to bear in mind the following important point. During the reunion at the airport, the mutual love for one another, the invisible bond, was obviously already there. What was already long-standing wanted to express itself anew and physically. It may also happen, though, that such a mutual love is expressed for the very first time, such as in the first tenderness, the first kiss, the first embrace. In this instance nothing that was long given is deepened and renewed, but something new begins.

Paul, sociologists would call my above examples "communication," and they too would distinguish between the external and internal side of each such communication. Furthermore, they would note that communication is always and without any exception mediated by signs, of which language is but one of many. Finally, they would assert that signs reinforce and deepen communication but also can open a channel of communication.

Allow me to take this one step further. In Jesus's life,

signs played an equally important role. Time and again
Jesus healed sick individuals. But how did he heal them?
By touching them and by laying his hands on them. He
also put his fingers into the ears of the deaf and made a
paste from earth and saliva and spread it onto the eyes
of the blind man. Jesus not only healed the sick but also
embraced and blessed children. He ate with tax collectors
and sinners, washed the feet of his disciples, and celebrated
Passover with them at the Last Supper.

All of these signs deeply affect the bodily nature of
humans, and we take them very seriously. Yet with Jesus,
these bodily gestures are always accompanied by the
word. The word, which itself is a sign, a *linguistic* sign,
removes the indetermination and ambiguity from these
bodily gestures. With Jesus, sign and word constitute a
unity. Thus, everything he does already has a sacramental
core structure. Jesus's deeds already lay the foundations
for the sacraments. After Easter we see unfolding what
the earthly Jesus had begun, and the sacraments become
the communication between the Risen Christ and the
Christians.

This encounter, this communication, is enacted in
signs, in symbolic actions and the word accompanying the
sign-act. Everyone receiving a sacrament encounters Christ
and is taken into the life, the death, and the resurrection of
Jesus Christ.

This should also now clearly demonstrate that to
speak of a sacrament being *only* a sign or *only* a symbol
is not only naive but outright foolish. Real encounters,
truly becoming one, for us in this world can happen only
through signs. (At this point I want to emphasize once
more that language also always belongs to this set of signs.)
Just imagine a marriage in which the partners no longer
talk to each other, haven't exchanged a word in days, a
marriage devoid of any kind or compassionate glance,
no tenderness, no touch, no kiss, no embrace. This is a

marriage that will soon end or is already at an end. Signs are vital for human beings, and without them we couldn't exist. Signs open communication and always facilitate new encounters.

The sacraments are part of this all-pervading world of signs. Thus, sacraments are something inherently human; they are inalienable as they enable encounters between the Risen Christ and those who believe. They are the bridge between the visible and the invisible, between time and eternity.

Allow me to make my own objection at this point. If the sacrament is a true encounter, true union with God through the Risen Lord, how can the human being presume such an encounter for him- or herself, such a union with the Risen One? In my imagined scene at the airport, it was two *human beings* coming together, on the same flight level, so to speak. Each one of them brought their love to the encounter, and both were in equal measure givers and receivers.

Can't we say the same in view of our encounter with Christ through the sacrament? Are we really partners? Or are we not simply and exclusively receivers? May we conceive of this encounter in the same vein as with our other customary encounters? Did we not overlook something fundamental?

I would consider such an objection to be not only justified but necessary, because it can help us to be more precise about what we have established so far. In a human encounter such as the one I described, someone can break the ice and hug the other with all his heart. That is different with a sacrament, as we cannot take the initiative here. We cannot say, "I want to meet Christ now." This encounter with Christ is something no human being can initiate, effect, trigger, or force to happen by any means. It is always granted as a gift. After all, how can we, of our own volition, attain the reality of the Risen One, even if he is always and everywhere close to us?

It is for the Risen One to take the initiative and facilitate the encounter. The sacraments are graces; they are gifts that the Risen Lord makes to us. For this very reason, each sacrament requires an administrator, as I cannot myself administer baptism or confirmation to myself. And I certainly cannot absolve myself from my sins. I need to see a priest* and let myself be absolved and freed from my guilt through the sacrament. The priest stands in for Christ to demonstrate that the sacrament of reconciliation with God is, like all sacraments, a gift that I cannot give to myself.

Likewise, it is impossible for me to grant or bestow the sacrament. They are bestowed and instated by Christ. This also clearly demonstrates that it is not *we* who effect the encounter with the Risen One, nor can *we* initiate the communication. We cannot open the door into the world of the Risen One.

Having said this, we should not imagine Christ bestowing these sacraments as if he were instating each sacrament in a kind of juridical act. Jesus certainly did not do this, and it was also not necessary. What he set in motion was the Church as the newly gathered eschatological Israel. This Church, in turn, is itself sacramental reality. The Church itself is a sacrament, and all sacraments are nothing but enactments of the Church's essence. I will address this in the letters on the individual sacraments.

This letter has again turned out far too long. Why do professors find it so hard to keep things short? I must close and can only tell you of my joy to hear that you have finally found soulmates among the churchgoers. It is so good to read that you connected with the Williams family and their children, Anthony and Mary.

How nice that the evening barbecue with them went so well, and you could learn so much more about your parish. And isn't it great that they even have a choir with such a good and esteemed choirmaster? So, your wife is already considering joining? Good to hear also of the various family circles. I'm sure you can talk about educational matters and pray together there. I knew for certain that God would not leave you alone and am really interested to hear what comes next.

With all the best greetings, also to the Williams family.

Letter 29

ADMISSION INTO THE CHURCH

Dear Beth,

This letter is about baptism. Your husband was not baptized, as he grew up in a home that wanted nothing to do with the Church. You yourself were baptized, but your parents viewed the baptism of their child more as a family occasion celebrating the start of a new life. Much the same was true for your first communion, which also turned out to be a dignified celebration among the family. Things were slightly different with your daughter Anna, as she herself decided to be baptized and you as her parents went along in silent amazement. You have supported and even shouldered the budding faith of your daughter ever since. It is high time, then, that I tell you something about this vital sacrament. What are the origins of the Christian baptism? Why does it exist and what does it mean?

Christian baptism has its origins in the baptismal practice of John. This last great prophet of Israel made his public appearance on the shore along the River Jordan and vigorously called on Israel to repent and turn around radically. But John the Baptist not only preached and warned his listeners of impending judgment. Those who came to him publicly confessed their sins and were subsequently immersed in the waters of the Jordan (Mark 1:4–5). The waters were a telling sign in this process as they sealed the baptized candidate against the judgment by fire that John the Baptist had proclaimed (Matt 3:7, 11).

There were many people from Israel who came to John the Baptist for baptism. One of them was Jesus, who did so in sincere solidarity with what he saw happening. Obviously, the Baptist's public teaching and actions triggered something vital in Jesus, for he understood that God was now acting on his people. It was about regathering the people of Israel. This was the hour to repent, as it was the hour for the new creation of the people of God.

Jesus, however, did not stay long with John the Baptist and his disciples at the Jordan. Jesus went to the villages and communities of Galilee, where he proclaimed the gospel of God's kingdom. In his preaching, Jesus adopted the Baptist's call to repent but gave it a different emphasis. His call was to repentance, not out of fear of impending judgment, but out of joy in God's kingdom.

After the Easter events, the disciples of Jesus continued in the vein initiated by the Baptist and Jesus, and called on Israel to repent. In the Acts of the Apostles, Luke offers a masterful account of Jesus's call for repentance in chapters 2—5. What strikes you instantly is that those who joined Jesus's disciples and believed their testimony were baptized, not necessarily in the Jordan, but where a flowing waterway or a clean water source was to be found (Acts 8:36–38).

This can be explained only by reference to the baptism practice of John the Baptist. As in his case, it was all about a radical turnaround and the eschatological renewal of Israel. Nonetheless, one key element had changed, as baptism now was administered "in the name of Jesus Christ" (Acts 2:38). This means that baptism now included all the salvation and reconciliation that had come with Jesus. It included the joy of the gospel, the redemption brought by Jesus's death, and the strength born out of his resurrection. Baptism presupposed a confession to Jesus Christ, which meant that anyone who had themselves been baptized took part in Jesus. Such a candidate was immersed into Israel's renewal and became a partaker in the new creation of the people of God.

As I pointed out earlier, the Christian faith is not primarily a teaching, a doctrine, or a collection of truths; one must learn to become a Christian. It is first and foremost an entry into a history that started with Abraham and found its fulfillment in Jesus Christ. This is all very evident from looking at baptism.

Those who are baptized also let themselves be called out with Abraham from the pagan world. They let themselves be liberated with Moses from the bondage of Egypt. They are taken into the covenant with God together with Israel at Mount Sinai. They are struck as they hear Israel's prophets' call to repent. They hear the gospel that Jesus proclaims, and they let themselves be freed and redeemed with the many whom Jesus healed from their compulsions and illnesses. And they receive a share in Jesus's death and resurrection.

Paul virtually interprets baptism as dying with Christ, so that the baptized can then live in Jesus as a new person (Rom 6:3–11). The baptized have left behind their old life and already partake in the new world that is dawning with Christ. This is also why Paul can say, "If anyone is in Christ, there is a new creation: everything old has passed away; see, everything has become new!" (2 Cor 5:17).

It is not just Paul's letters that bespeak this awareness that one has entered a new creation and a new social order with the acceptance of the faith. The entire early Church was carried by this awareness and was acutely aware of the great significance of baptism. Baptism was deemed a change of rule. It was a renunciation of the gods and demons of pagan society and entry into the Church, the realm of Christ's rule.

All of this was enacted in concrete terms. Probably as early as the second century, the baptismal candidate had to provide a guarantor who vouched for the sincerity of the candidate's conversion. What's more, the candidate had to attend a three-year baptism preparation course, which provided a careful introduction into Judeo-Christian knowledge of discernment and the life of faith.

It was self-evident to the early Church that baptismal candidates would not automatically acquire an imbued knowledge of Christian life but had to learn it. It also knew full well that evil is strong and mighty and that one had to fight tooth and nail for every foothold in God's kingdom. That is also why the instructions for the baptismal candidates and baptism itself were accompanied by symbolic acts vividly portraying this battle. They are the ceremonial renunciation of evil, confession of faith, laying on of hands, descent into the baptismal font, and ascent out of the water.

It was therefore only logical that nothing in the life of the newly baptized could remain as before. Many pagan professions were no longer possible for Christians, namely, all those that involve them with pagan myths and cults. As teachers had to use texts full of stories about the gods, as sculptors and painters had to depict gods, and as civil servants had to swear their oath in the name of these gods, none of these professions could be performed by Christians. The same was true for actors, gladiators, prostitutes and their procurers, astrologers, and dream readers. All of these were admitted as baptismal candidates only if they gave up their professions.

It was equally frowned upon to visit stage plays, gladiatorial contests, or animal fights; to participate in processions or parades associated with heathen cult rituals; or to partake in public feasts on imperial holidays. Even common idiomatic expressions as "by Jove" were to be avoided. This list of Christian refusals could be extended for quite some length.

However, it was much more important for the newly baptized to grow into a community in which people shared and joined their lives, carried each other's burdens, and acted responsibly to and for one another. What the early Christian Church called *agapē* was a state of being no longer for oneself but for God and the brothers and sisters in the communities. It was experienced as a radical new beginning, away from a former pagan existence, and as the gift of new life.

We certainly also must admit that this new existence after baptism was not proactively lived by all the baptized. The awareness that death had already taken place through baptism and that physical death at the hands of persecutors no longer held any power over one was by no means so strong among all Christians that they had overcome their fear of dying. During the Decian persecutions, meted out by the Roman emperor in the years AD 250–51, the Church had to face the fact that large numbers of its believers showed no loyalty to their faith but rather obeyed the emperor's edict and partook in the sacrifices to the gods as decreed for the entire Roman Empire. Others resorted to bribery to obtain certificates showing they had participated in the sacrifices.

The dismay over the true nature of its communities, however, showed the Church how alive the awareness still was that the faithful as an entity should have refused the emperor's edict.

The fourth century finally saw an end to the persecution under the emperors Galerius and Constantine. The Church gradually turned into the imperial Church, and it became routine to be a Christian. There was no choice anymore, but one had to be a Christian and had to be baptized. As late as the nineteenth century, after the Age of Enlightenment and the institution of religious liberty, Christian baptism and Christian existence remained the norm for many families in many parts of the world.

Only the twentieth century saw a radical shift in this situation. Today, the Christian faith is no longer self-evident. In many countries, such as Japan, China, India, and the predominantly Muslim countries, it had never been so. Now, however, we can see Christians slowly becoming a minority in formerly Christian countries. Added to this we can also see something else. Well over fifty countries document persecution of Christians on a scale not even seen in the Roman Empire. Elsewhere, although Christians are not persecuted outright, we can see the Church being ridiculed or met with utter indifference.

I sometimes wonder whether this is a bad or a good development. It is always bad if people are isolated, disadvantaged, hurt, or murdered because of their faith. It might be good, on the other hand, if Christians are forced to reconsider their faith under such circumstances, for this faith is no longer self-evident but requires Christians to distance themselves from false role models, false behavior, false "gods." It demands a clear and conscious existence borne out of faith. It demands that they make their own decisions, and that is a good thing.

Many kind regards to all of you
and the Williams family.

Letter 30

STRENGTHENED THROUGH THE HOLY SPIRIT

Dear Paul,

You quoted from my last letter that "faith requires that one makes one's own decision" to follow this up by an often-voiced opinion stating, "Baptism also requires a free decision, which makes the baptism of babies and children before the age of consent fundamentally wrong."

I am with you on the first part of the sentence, that "baptism requires a free decision." You are right on this. This is also the very reason why the sacrament of baptism is complemented by the sacrament of confirmation. That confirmation is the necessary addition to baptism is evident from looking at the history of the sacrament of baptism. In the early Church, mostly adults were baptized, even though infant baptism must have been a practice from the earliest beginnings. The New Testament lists several instances of someone being baptized along with their entire household (Acts 16:15; 1 Cor 1:16). This means that they were baptized together with the entire family and hence also with their children. Normally, though, baptism in the early Church was for adults.

The practice was that as soon as the candidate had made their baptismal profession of faith in God the Father, the Son, and the Holy Spirit and had risen from the water, the bishop* laid his hands on them and called down the Holy Spirit upon them. Next, they were anointed with consecrated oil, received the kiss of peace from the bishop, and exchanged that kiss of peace with the entire congregation. The invocation of the Holy Spirit was an integral part of the baptism just administered. Baptism and confirmation were one ritual entity that signified acceptance into the Church.

It was only in the following centuries that changes were gradually made. Baptism and the invocation of the Holy Spirit were administered at two different ages, so that they developed into two distinct sacraments. Nonetheless, they remained assigned to each other, as confirmation is the fulfillment of baptism and is its vitally necessary addition, because it is true that an infant cannot yet say, "Yes, I want to be baptized," or "No, I don't want to be baptized," or even, "I want to wait a little longer before baptism." Consequently, it is only with confirmation that what was begun in baptism becomes a sacrament received as a *free decision*.

Anyone who decides in favor of confirmation thus says, "Yes, I stand by my baptism. I say yes to being a Christian. I want to live as a Christian. I have recognized that it is good to believe in God and Jesus Christ. I now affirm what happened to me in baptism by saying yes in full freedom and before God and the whole congregation. I publicly profess my faith and ask God to grant me his Holy Spirit that I may live a truly Christian life."

Beth, you will surely respond, "For heaven's sake! If that is so, why does one baptize infants, who are totally unaware of what is being done to them? Why not

wait until they can decide for themselves in freedom?"
Put differently: Why are baptism and confirmation not
administered today as they were back then, at a point
in time when the candidate is old enough to make an
informed decision in true freedom? Is the practice of infant
baptism then not some form of violation? Should not every
child first grow up free from any religious education?

My answer is that one should imagine in concrete
detail what it would be like if parents never talked to their
children about God, never prayed with them, never spoke
of Jesus to them, never attended a Church service with
them. If one asked them, "Why do you do it this way?"
they would reply, "When our children turn eighteen, they
can decide for themselves whether or not they want to
become Christians. Up to that age they should grow up
completely neutrally so that they can really decide freely
once their time comes."

The whole thing is absurd. Believing in God, trusting
in God, speaking to God, confessing to God, all that
needs to be learned the way one learns to speak or brush
one's teeth. If you've never learned how to communicate
with God, if you are left utterly without any idea about
God, you will not be able to decide for or against God
later. Though faith is pure grace and a gift, it still has a
human side to it, which one can experience and grow into.
Obviously, it can happen that God surprises us and draws
us suddenly and unprepared and without any prerequisites
into the faith. Yet aren't those parents who themselves
believe in God, but keep their children away from God for
the sake of their freedom, like parents who don't give their
children any food?

Now you might answer to this, "Alright, apart from
the exaggeration of a completely neutral parenting style,
let's have the child raised in the faith, with all the aspects
of faith, but the sacrament should come at the end of this
process rather than at the beginning." To which I reply that

this would be conceivable, of course, and there are actually Christian communities that practice exactly this. The question is just, why not have a sacramental form to begin this process of growing into the faith? This would express in a very visible way that faith and baptism are not just free decisions but also a matter of purest grace, given by God and completely unmerited.

Infant baptism is then the grace-steeped beginning of a wider process as it means entering into a long history of faith, in which many are intertwined: the parents, the godparents, believing friends and acquaintances, the entire community. Over time, decision-making will mature, and the first steps will be taken on one's own feet. There comes the point when parents can no longer decide for their child and when they no longer have the right to do so. This is when the free affirmative yes can be said to everything that had started with baptism. It may also turn out to be no. The parents, however, must always, and right from the very beginning, be cautious and tactful in all matters concerning the faith of their child. There must never be any coercion in matters of the faith.

Paul, you will have sensed already that the actual developmental history from baptism to confirmation is long and rich in facets. The real question is not so much one of infant baptism but whether there is a faithful family of believers around the child that forms the basis for infant baptism. The follow-up, associated question would then be, how do you prepare for and administer confirmation? To me this seems to be the second problem, because over the last two centuries confirmation has mutated into a kind of rite of passage into adulthood in large sections of the Church. This has "gentrified" confirmation and often removed it far from what it means for the faith and a Christian existence.

Like all sacraments, though, confirmation is an encounter with Jesus Christ. Anyone really meeting

Strengthened through the Holy Spirit

Christ cannot remain neutral or indifferent. Either one positions oneself in opposition to Christ or one makes oneself available to Christ. In the latter case, one will ask what one can do in support of the gospel, for the build-up of community, as a service to the Church. This can be very different for every individual, as everyone has their very own calling. It is always a life for God in the Church, though. Dear Paul, thank you very much for continuing to ask and not giving up.

Kindest greetings to you all.

Letter 31

TABLE COMMUNITY WITH JESUS

Dear Beth,

Your last letter shows clearly that your family is going through a little turbulence right now. Your husband is seriously considering whether it is time to be baptized. You are all for it and so is Anna, but your husband is still wavering. He says that he can only imagine a baptism in the very smallest of settings, certainly not during a Sunday Mass in front of the whole congregation. At times, your family discussions over this are very serious and sober, and at other times full of joy and confidence.

This confidence has been strengthened by your growing friendship with the Williams family. If I read correctly between the lines, it appears that Anna has befriended ten-year-old Mary and fourteen-year-old Anthony. Anthony especially is urging Anna to let bygones be bygones and rejoin the altar servers. He says he wants to look after her in the group, which naturally delights Anna. Let's see how all this works out!

In my last letter I had outlined how the early Church had put baptism together with confirmation as the sacraments of initiation bestowed upon admission into the Church. However, this initiation also included a third sacrament: holy communion, the reception of the Eucharist.

Before I continue, I need to explain what is meant by the word *Eucharist*. It is Greek and means simply "thanksgiving." In the Catholic Church, communion is regularly received during Mass* and is tied to the great thanksgiving of the Eucharistic Prayer*. The Eucharistic Prayer is the most important and solemn prayer of the Church, in which the priest gives thanks on behalf of the entire gathered community to God for everything God has done for his people through Jesus Christ.

The Eucharistic Prayer begins with the invitation, "Lift up your hearts," to which the congregation responds, "We lift them up to the Lord." The priest continues, "Let us give thanks to the Lord our God," followed by the congregation's answer, "It is right and just." This solemn prayer is the culmination of the Mass, as it repeats the words Jesus said during the Last Supper. As it is the Church's greatest expression of gratitude, the entire celebratory assembly, with the Liturgy of the Word and the believers' reception of holy communion, is called the "celebration of the Eucharist*," while the bread the faithful receive is called "bread of the Eucharist." So much on the etymology of the term!

The practice in the early Church was for the baptismal applicants to receive both baptism and confirmation during the Easter Vigil, after which they were then taken to the celebration of the Eucharist, where, together with the entire community, they received the Eucharist for the first time. This first-time reception of communion amid the community marked the completion of their entry into the Church. Now they were fully connected to Christ, for which there is no more meaningful expression than the shared meal in table community with Christ. What is the history of this table meal?

The meal of the Eucharist goes back to Jesus's Last Supper before his death, which was a Jewish Seder* celebrated on the eve of Passover*. For this meal, the entire family would gather and eat the paschal lamb*. Jesus, however, did not celebrate his last Seder with his family, as was customary, or with a collection of friends. Jesus celebrated it with the twelve disciples he had chosen as a sign to indicate that for him it was all about gathering and renewing Israel. The twelve disciples symbolized the twelve tribes of Israel.

The central element of the Seder is the recollection of God's great deed of liberation, the remembrance of the night when Israel fled out of Egypt. In the descriptions of this Seder by Matthew, Mark, Luke, and Paul, we find that the celebration of this remembrance is something natural, though they do not specifically mention or describe the Seder ritual Jesus celebrated with the twelve disciples. Instead, these Last Supper narratives tell us something else that was special and new.

During the meal Jesus takes the bread, says a prayer of grace over it, breaks it, and passes it to the twelve. All of this is still the predefined rite as it is the grace said before the main meal. What is special is the interpretation Jesus gives the broken bread that he shares among the twelve: "Take, eat; this is my body" (Matt 26:26; Mark 14:22). This is an extremely concise interpretation, which we can only read as: "I myself am this bread. This is me with my history and my life. My life will be broken like this bread. I give it to you so that you may have a share in me and my death."

This symbolic act is first a prophecy of his own death, as Jesus uses the symbol of the broken bread to foretell that he will die a violent death. Yet, this symbolic act is more than just the foretelling of his own death. With it, Jesus gives the twelve a share in his existence, which is given over into death. His death has a dimension of profundity, which the twelve, and with them Israel—for the twelve represent the twelve tribes of Israel—are to receive a share in and partake of.

The New Testament's descriptions of the Last Supper presuppose that Jesus's prayer of grace and his interpretation of the broken bread will be followed by the main course: the eating of the paschal lamb. At the end of the main course the father of the house would hold up the so-called cup of grace and once more say a prayer of thanksgiving. Jesus also follows this ritual and gives it a new dimension.

In the narrative of Mark's Gospel, Jesus blesses the cup with these words: "This is my blood of the covenant, which is poured out for many" (Mark 14:24). In Luke the interpretation over the cup reads, "This cup that is poured out for you is the new covenant in my blood" (Luke 22:20).

Thus, Jesus refers anew to his impending death, interpreting the red wine to be his blood that will soon be spilled. "Spilling blood" of course is a byword for murder, as Jesus will be killed. It is more than just a prophecy of death, however. Mark alludes to the "blood of the covenant," which is a reference to Exodus 24:4–8, which records the founding act of Israel at Mount Sinai in its covenant agreement with God. When this covenant is sealed, Moses sprinkles the blood of sacrificed animals over a stone altar.

Against this Old Testament background, Jesus's word over the cup of grace clearly reveals that his life will be given over to death. His blood, which will be spilled in the process, will not be shed in vain and senselessly. Instead, it is the "blood of the covenant," which means that it renews and fulfills the covenant God once made with Israel at Mount Sinai. In Jesus's death, the people of God are created anew through the blood of Jesus, which frees Israel from its sin and grants it atonement*.

A central aspect of the Last Supper passages is also the instruction to repeat the enactment: "Do this in remembrance of me" (Luke 22:19; 1 Cor 11:24–25). The verb *do* means here "to enact, undertake, celebrate." And the proactive "remembrance" of Jesus's death means more than just "remembering." Whenever the remembrance of Jesus's Last Supper is renewed, we make present Jesus's death as well as the salvation effected through his death.

Beth, surely you sense that whenever the Church assembles to celebrate the Eucharist, it is unlike any human gathering, of which there are thousands. Rather, in these gatherings the Last Supper, which Jesus celebrated with the twelve as representatives of Israel, is made present. All of us are then assembled around Jesus in that Upper Room of the Last Supper. We receive a share and partake in his suffering, in his death, and in his resurrection. And we even receive our share in Israel's history because Jesus's Seder is incomprehensible without the exodus story.

It is important that you both keep in mind the Old Testament and the Jewish tradition of the Eucharist, because without that background, the eating of the bread at communion is dangerously close to magic. The host, the small wafer that Christians consume during the celebration of the Eucharist, is not some kind of invigorating medicinal potion. Communion is an immediate encounter with Jesus Christ. By celebrating the Eucharist and eating the eucharistic host, we receive a share in Jesus himself as well as in his history.

There is another misconception that we must guard against. It is a misconception that is not limited to receiving the Eucharist but affects all the sacraments. In an earlier letter, I had written that the sacraments were "signs." So far so good. The word *sign*, however, is immediately falsified if we say they are "merely" signs. This would mean they are just a form of figurative illustration or reassurance but would in themselves have no effect. What bestows salvation on to us would be solely and exclusively the faith, while the sacraments would just be subsequent elucidations and illustrations, mementos for what has already occurred during the consummation of the faith.

However, this position fails to do justice to the Christian sacraments and above all to the celebration of the Eucharist. Anyone celebrating the Eucharist is celebrating not a visualization but, together with Jesus, the meal before his death and has real table communion with Jesus. Obviously, faith is integral to every sacrament, but the sacrament is more than a didactic visualization exercise. In and through the sacrament we encounter Jesus Christ himself. What happens during this meal is the high point and culmination of all sacramental life and is the heart of the life of the Church.

I wish you and your husband a deep longing for the grace to receive this sacrament at some point (perhaps soon?) and send you my most heartfelt greetings.

Letter 32

REPENTANCE AND HEALING

Dear Paul,

Anna has returned to serving at the altar and suddenly she doesn't find Mass dull anymore. What a joy to read this! I can see her before my inner eye as she joins Anthony Williams for the collection* of the offerings. She must have been very proud.

Something in Anna has been healed that was deeply wounded, and many people helped in this healing process to set things straight again. You and your wife, the parish priest who immediately found the time for a talk, the girls and boys ready and willing to listen, and in the end of course also Anthony, who played such a vital role. The whole process was extremely important for Anna, and we cannot really appreciate fully how much this immediate experience of "reconciliation" means for her life.

But aren't we all in need of such reconciliation, remediation, and healing? After all, we do not only commit "trivial offenses," misdemeanors, and follies. We are not just the reason awkward embarrassments keep resurfacing for years, leaving a stale taste in our own memories. And we do not just have habits apt to constantly offend others. If only that was all there is!

No, there is real guilt and sin in our lives. There are the good things we should have done but failed to do. There are the deep wounds we inflicted on others. There is breach of trust, slander, deep-seated pride, and terrible situations when we ignored and violated the freedom and dignity of others. There is greed, avarice, egotism, cold-heartedness, and indifference. Who could claim to be free from them all?

Baptism has liberated Christians from the power of evil and the calamitous entanglements in which we are all caught up. Baptism has taken Christians into the Church and with that into the freedom and clarity of Jesus Christ. No longer are they subjugated by sin, as baptism has immersed them in the unfathomable mercy of God's love. They could now live this love themselves.

Yet those moments I described above, moments of cold lovelessness, greed, and pride, keep cropping up, and often they are not merely moments. Evil can gain ground again within us. So this is our situation and why at the beginning of every celebration of the Eucharist the congregation confesses their sins and asks God for forgiveness of their sins.

There are plenty more opportunities to ask God for forgiveness, such as a spontaneous apology when you notice that you've done wrong and the evening soul-searching as you look back on what the day had brought. We can repent whenever we notice how far away we have strayed from the gospel. In particular, the forty days of Lent before Easter give us the opportunity to repent together with the entire Church. Over and above all this, there is the *sacrament* of penance, forgiveness, reconciliation, remediation, and healing. Why? I'll give you two reasons:

Every marriage, as you will surely agree, Paul, has situations where one partner has hurt the other, wounded and done the other wrong. Now, one could inwardly ask the other for forgiveness with the intention of never letting it happen again. This is certainly possible. It is not always necessary to talk it over, expand on it, and squeeze everything out of oneself. Every good marriage has such room for mutual understanding in which there is no need for words and the signals transmitted are understood.

However, by the same token, in every shared relationship there will be situations in which one must speak one's mind and ask for forgiveness. In this case, significantly more happens than if one were to bear it silently. If you were to resort to only silent contrition in such situations, you might be cruelly mistaken. You might not even comprehend the extent of damage you have done in the first place. Only the verbal admission of one's own guilt *before the wronged one* leads to the whole truth.

Much the same happens during confession*. I am not settling something with God purely within myself, but I confess my guilt within the sphere of the Church because the priest who absolves me from my sins does so on behalf of the Church. As I confess my guilt before a delegate of the Church, I give that guilt its full weight. I no longer play down my sin as a triviality soon forgotten and gone. Moreover, every grave sin destroys something of the splendor and beauty of the Church. Thus, the healing of sins is also elementary to the Church and is the first reason why the sacrament of reconciliation exists as confession to a priest.

There is also a second reason: Like all sacraments, confession anticipates what will happen to us in death as we come before the face of God. Baptism grants us a share

in eternal life. Receiving the Eucharist already heralds
the beginning of the eternal feast before God that will
know no end. During confession, then, we place ourselves
under God's judgment, which we will face at our death
in any case. In confession I already stand before Christ; it
is Christ's merciful judgment over my sins, and I shall be
freed from my sins. Confession is God's offer to me to use
this moment and hour to reestablish the grace of baptism
and start out anew and free from sin. The absolution the
priest pronounces after the confession of sins, says,

> God, the Father of mercies, through the death and
> resurrection of his Son has reconciled the world to
> himself and sent the Holy Spirit among us for the
> forgiveness of sins. Through the ministry of the
> Church may God give you pardon and peace. And
> I absolve you from your sins in the name of the
> Father, and of the Son, and of the Holy Spirit.

Here Christians are given a gift of great freedom and
profound joy. It is as great as the joy two people experience
when they have been reconciled to one another, and their
love has grown deeper and stronger in the process. There
is nothing more liberating than to be fully reconciled with
God. It is an integral part of the coming of the kingdom of
God, which is why Jesus not only preached the kingdom
of God but went to the guilty and sinful, ate with them,
conferred on them God's forgiveness, and freed them from
their guilt.

I encourage you to read the parable of the prodigal
son in Luke 15:11–32, for it shows that reconciliation
with God is like emerging out of the misery of sin, like
rediscovering home, like a feast.

Paul, in one of your letters you wrote that
environmental protection and the preservation of creation
are very dear to you. Allow me therefore to conclude with

a thought that is certainly related to this. Every repentance by a human being, every confession of sin before God, and every remediation that follows on such a confession of sins restores a piece of destroyed creation. God wants nothing but for his creation to be unhurt and unharmed.

I greet all of you with all my heart and wish above all Anna much joy and happiness when serving at the altar.

Letter 33

SALVATION FOR THE SICK AND DYING

Dear Beth,

Your brother wrote you a long letter, which you tell me was very defensive. Here's my interpretation of the situation: Your brother clearly loves you very much and regrets that he can't see eye to eye with his own sister. At the same time, he feels that he cannot change his position in matters of the faith. So he tries to enlist your understanding and to uphold your mutually good relationship.

And it should remain good. I think you should write to him and tell him that this has not changed in the least. Most importantly, encourage him to keep searching so honestly for the truth about the world and life, without becoming bitter and cynical, because then he is also already on the path to God, as God is truth. If I were you, I would not venture into any discussions, unless he directly asks concrete questions. Once that happens, answer him, and I'll gladly assist you.

Let's return to the sacraments. I had said toward the end of my letter on confession that this sacrament is also founded on Jesus's deeds, specifically his encounters with outcasts and sinners. The same applies for the sacrament of anointing of the sick. Jesus healed sick people again and again, whether they were blind, deaf, crippled, or lepers. It was the many healing miracles that caused his name to spread throughout Israel.

Of course, Jesus's acts of healing are linked with his proclamation of God's kingdom. Because the kingdom of God comes through him and his gospel, everything in Israel must change, because life in God's kingdom is imaginable only as healed life.

There are many dimensions to such "healed life." It can mean being cured of a disease, but it can also mean to heal inwardly, coming to peace and quiet, laying one's whole life in God's hands, or making peace with God and humanity, and *in this way* becoming healed.

The path there leads through repentance and turning away from ingrained ideas and behavioral patterns toward God's saving thoughts. These different dimensions of "healing" are important because it is not just a matter of nursing the body back to health but also of healing life, as well as one's own history. We all carry so many burdens with us, whether they are wounds, injuries, and insults, unspoken and unsettled issues, unredeemed and unresolved matters, confusion, or, above all, the guilt that weighs on us. All these afflict us in our illnesses and darken the splendor of the kingdom of God. All this needs healing.

The New Testament describes how Jesus's healing acts continue after his death and resurrection through his disciples, who not only *visit* the sick and *comfort* them, but actually *heal* them. The Acts of the Apostles provides a whole series of such healings. I recommend that you and your husband read, for example, Acts 3:1–10. This passage shows that even after Easter, the apostles took Jesus's words seriously: "As you go, proclaim the good news, 'The kingdom of heaven has come near.' Cure the sick, raise the dead, cleanse the lepers, cast out demons" (Matt 10:7–8).

Over the centuries, the Church always knew that this healing mandate was central to her very essence. And from the beginning, the Church cared for the sick and infirm. Hospitals were invented by the Church, and countless monastic apothecaries provided the sick with medicine grown and extracted from their gardens. St. Hildegard of Bingen combined tender care of the sick with exact observation of the efficacy of medicinal remedies, and she was by no means alone in her work.

All of this demonstrates that the sacrament of anointing of the sick is embedded in a broader spectrum of attentive care, a care that really aims to offer humankind holistic healing. Obviously, medicine has its rightful place in this, and a good, advanced medical system mutually complements sacramental care for the sick.

I will not go into the details of how the sacrament is administered to the sick, as your last letter gave a moving account of it. It was good that all three of you attended the ceremony for Grandmother Williams two weeks ago. You wrote that her condition had suddenly deteriorated so she received the sacrament. You saw with your own eyes how the priest anointed her forehead and hands with the special oil for the sick, which a bishop had blessed. And you were also there when she received holy communion. It is good to hear that she is getting better. By the way, this was much the same with my mother, who literally "came to life again" after receiving the anointing of the sick.

Obviously, things can also be different, and then the sacrament becomes a healing seal on a life. The dying give their entire life, their whole history with everything that has happened to them, into God's merciful hands. Whenever this is possible, it is indeed a great grace. It is at once deeply human and deeply Christian if the entire family gathers around the deathbed and if the dying person can take a last silent breath under the prayer of the attending relatives.

You may pray for such a parting hour, for it is a gift, and the sacrament of anointing of the sick becomes the extreme unction. This certainly doesn't change the fact that originally, this sacrament was intended for the living, as it fulfills Jesus's mandate to us to heal the sick. There shouldn't really be any sickness, as it is a calamity. God wants life and is a God of life.

I greet you all very warmly and kindly ask you to extend my best wishes to Grandma Williams.

Letter 34

ACTING WITH THE AUTHORITY OF JESUS

Dear Paul,

My last letters will have made it clear that the sacraments are rooted in Israel and above all in Jesus, in whom the eschatological Israel has already become reality. The sacrament of baptism goes back to John the Baptist's practice at the River Jordan, which Jesus also underwent. The sacrament of confirmation goes back to the Holy Spirit, which Jesus received in baptism and handed down to his disciples on the day of Pentecost. The Eucharist is based on the Jewish Seder evening and Jesus's words and deeds during his Last Supper. The sacrament of reconciliation originates in Jesus's treatment of sinners and outcasts, while the anointing of the sick goes back to his many healing miracles.

So does the sacrament of priestly ordination also originate in Jesus and his practice of God's kingdom? This could certainly not be said, if one requires that Jesus would have had to ordain priests, dressed the newly ordained in chasubles*, and handed them breviaries* and a book of canon law. However, it is nonsensical to argue on such a level. The sacraments are a consummation of Jesus's bequest to the Church. They had to develop over the course of centuries, had to be realized, unfold, and take up their specific forms. They even had to define and delineate themselves against misuse and heresies. So no one can insist that we should find them, fully formed, in Jesus himself.

The same applies to ordination, the essence of which is already fully consummated by Jesus. Its defining feature is the mission, the *sending out* of the disciples to the people of God. Jesus sent out the twelve to proclaim the kingdom of God in Israel (Mark 6:7ff.).

This proclamation of God's kingdom was not just limited to proclaiming the good news but also included testifying to the kingdom of God by caring for sinners and the sick. The twelve were to do as Jesus had done. They acted on the authority of Jesus himself (Matt 10:1).

Acting on Jesus's authority means that what they do is not from their own strength, their own talents, or the specific skills of the people of God, as if they were a crucible of these. What they do is solely and exclusively on the strength of their mandate from Jesus. He gives them authority to testify to God's kingdom in word and deed. And it is in this authority that they make Jesus present and manifest, that they represent him.

The delegation of the twelve and the official testimony inherent in this mission is the root of the Church office. Of course, this office had to find and develop its appropriate forms within the Church, but this process began very early. It already began to take shape within the New Testament communities. As early as the Acts of the Apostles and the letters to Timothy and Titus we can read that there were apostolic offices in the Church, as they speak of elders, bishops, and deacons*. And the New Testament communities already practiced the handing over of offices through the laying on of hands. Thus, today's bishops are connected to the time of the apostles by this long chain of the laying on of hands.

But let's leave aside all these historic facts, including Jesus's delegation of the twelve, and ask very simply, Why does there have to be any Church office at all and, what's more, an office that does not democratically execute the will of the majority but is bound by precedence? The answer is simply because of this precedent and because this precedent must be preserved, guarded, honored, and respected. It must be handed down and transmitted. It must stay alive.

By the way, these catchphrases "democratically" and "will of the majority" that I mentioned just now are a terrible simplification, because even the people's representatives in a democracy are not *solely* tied to the will of the people but also to their conscience. Moreover, they are bound by the relevant constitution and basic rights. So they couldn't just abolish these constitutional rights, even if the will of the people demands just that.

Even more, then, the people of God and the Church are strictly bound to basic tenets that are in no way at their free disposal. The fundamental tenet by which the Church lives is Jesus Christ, his proclamation of the gospel, his gathering of the people of God, his commandment of love, and his care and attention for the destitute poor and abandoned lonely. Over and above this, for the Church, the fundamental tenet is all that the Holy Spirit has taught her over the course of Church history (John 14:26). This is to what the Church office is bound, and the Church cannot abolish these, her fundamental tenets, nor can she dispose of them but must serve them with her power and strength.

Paul, allow me to illustrate what I have just written. When you are in Church on Sundays, you see the priest, the bishop's representative and delegate, wear a stole* and a chasuble. Why does he do so? Surely not so that the proceedings in church might take on a little splendor!

Nor is the color of the chasuble primarily intended to show unmistakably which liturgical season one is currently celebrating, whether it is Advent, Lent, Easter, or Ordinary Time. No, the vestments worn by the priest are meant to say that even if he presides over the service, he does not do so on his own authority or the authority of the congregated community, but on the authority of Jesus Christ. It is Jesus whom he is to make present.

Accordingly, when he preaches, he is not to expound on his private opinion, his private theological insights, or his favorite ideas for the reform of the Church, but he is to explain the Old Testament, interpret the apostolic letters, and proclaim the gospel. He is not there to aggrandize himself, but to give glory to God with everything he does. He must be very humble, because he does not create the Church—the Church is wholly the work of God. Therefore, the priest, like the faithful, again and again must confess his trespasses, his guilt, and his disrespect of God's glory. It is to signify this that the priest wears the chasuble and does not show up in suit and tie.

I have not yet said a word about the role of the so-called laity* in the Church, the countless women and men who are equally "delegated." They have received their mission through confirmation by the bishop. Every baptized and confirmed Christian is sent out to live as a Christian, testify to the gospel, and collaborate in building up community. There is no question about this at all, but this letter addresses the *official* mission. The Church needs both types of mission as she lives from them both.

The service Anna now provides almost every Sunday and occasionally on weekdays is also a service to the Church, and you may be glad that she does it with such devotion.

Kind greetings to you all!

Letter 35

SYMBOL OF GOD'S FAITHFULNESS

Dear Beth,

Is the sacrament of marriage also grounded in the Bible? The Old Testament certainly contains texts that accord great dignity to the partnership between man and woman. Right at the very beginning of the story of creation we read, "So God created humankind in his image, in the image of God he created them; male and female he created them" (Gen 1:27). A few lines on, the deep union between married partners is described as follows: "Therefore a man leaves his father and his mother and clings to his wife, and they become one flesh" (Gen 2:24).

In addition, a great number of prophets describe the covenant between God and Israel using the image of marital love. Israel repeatedly broke the covenant with its God, but God remained true to Israel with unswerving faithfulness (Isa 54:1–10).

The highly poetic Song of Songs of the Old Testament paints in vivid colors an image of a young man meeting his beloved. Just one such passage reads,

Set me as a seal upon your heart,
    as a seal upon your arm;
for love is strong as death,
    passion fierce as the grave.
Its flashes are flashes of fire,
    a raging flame.
Many waters cannot quench love,
    neither can floods drown it. (Song 8:6–7)

The decisive aspect of this is that the love poems of the Song of Songs made their way into the Old Testament only because they were understood as a description of the covenant between God and his people, with all the stages of losing oneself, searching, and finding oneself again, which were so integral to Israel's covenant history. We cannot even assume that these love songs were composed from the outset as an expression of the love between God and Israel.

The writers of the New Testament took up this exceptional topic and compared the depth of marital love with the love between Christ and the Church. Thus, the author of the letter to the community in Ephesus writes, "'For this reason a man will leave his father and mother and be joined to his wife, and the two will become one flesh.' This is a great mystery, and I am applying it to Christ and the church" (Eph 5:31–32).

Comparing marriage to God's covenant with Israel or to the connection between Christ and the Church shows clearly that marriage and marital love are held in high esteem. It comes hardly as a surprise, then, that Jesus is scandalously radical in his defense and protection of marriage! The man who even looks lustfully at a woman has already committed adultery and thus is guilty of a capital crime, Jesus says in the Sermon on the Mount (Matt 5:27–28). He is equally harsh in his condemnation of divorce: "Whoever divorces his wife and marries another commits adultery against her; and if she divorces her husband and marries another, she commits adultery" (Mark 10:11–12). Jesus justifies such indissolubility of marriage on the strength of Genesis 2:24. Here the two marriage partners become *one* flesh. "So they are no longer two, but *one* flesh. Therefore what God has joined together, let no one separate" (Mark 10:8–9).

This was as scandalous then as it is now. After all, aren't there marriages that are simply unbearable? Aren't there marriages that were entered into prematurely, without thought and realistic expectations? Moreover, the circumstances of life can change, and can't they make the continuation of a marriage seem doubtful? Doesn't today's longer life expectancy justify the right to a new relationship and new horizons? Isn't the insolubility of marriage, the way the New Testament teaches it, potentially a condemnation to life in confined and even servile circumstances?

It is perfectly fine to ask all of these questions, and a great deal could be said in reply. One central answer would be that a sacramental marriage must not turn into a reclusive and isolated relationship between two people. It has been sealed by the Church and has a right to the support of a Christian community. This help could be given when searching for an apartment, rearing children, or assisting in illness or financial distress. It is especially in these instances that the community, as with and for one another, should prove to be what it is by its very essence.

Above all, a marriage made before God and the Church may also count on God's help. The two spouses are never alone, but there is a third party present. They also have shared prayer and opportunities for confession and starting their marriage anew after dry patches and crises, because they have the possibility to reconcile.

The New Testament prohibition of divorce, or, better put, the commandment to remain faithful to one another

for life, basically highlights what Christian marriage is.
It is a union beyond the erotic and sexual, although that
also has its place. Sexuality, eros, and selfless love all must
permeate one another. The yes that the two partners
promise each other during the marriage ceremony means
"You with everything that you are!" at the same time as
it says, "Only you!" as well as "You forever," and "You in
good times and bad!"

The fact that we can enter such a bond is an essential
part of human nature and indeed constitutes its highest
dignity. By the way, the mutual trust and fidelity of their
parents gives children a sense of safety and secure comfort.
Think only of the uprooted displacement and misery that
children must endure when their parents separate!

We should not take the Christian divorce interdict
to be a heavy burden weighing down on spouses, but as
the place that reveals clearly and unambiguously what
Christian marriage is. It is more than a relationship in
nature, even though its natural foundations must never
be ignored. It is one of the highest cultural achievements,
mirroring God's faithfulness to his people. It is creative
love, a mandate to build up a community and to serve the
Church. I am quite deliberate in stating that last sentence,
although you hardly ever hear it anymore and it is almost
forgotten. Christian marriage is mandated with building
a community and serving the Church. The affirmative yes
spoken during a Church marriage ceremony means that
as well, and not just "You alone" or "You forever" but also
"Together with you for the gospel!"

Christian marriage is exposed to more erosion than
practically any other institution, for even the word *love* is
constantly cheapened by our societies. For naturalists it
is no more than a hormonal process, for the more hard-
nosed it is self-gratification in a twin-pack. For cynics it
is downgraded to a tedious habit once the first bloom has
wilted away.

Symbol of God's Faithfulness

There are other voices out there as well, though. The German philosopher Gottfried Wilhelm Leibniz, who also excelled as a formidable mathematician and skilled engineer, put it thus: "To love is to find pleasure in the happiness of others."

It is this joy I wish you, dear Beth, your husband, and daughter Anna.

Letter 36

LIFE FROM THE SACRAMENTS

Dear Beth and Paul,

This time, the two of you answered *together* in a very long letter that was one of your nicest and dearest. Though you were not married in the Church, your letter clearly indicates the views you held ten years ago when you got your marriage certificate from the registry office. The exceptionally happy marriages enjoyed by your parents played a key role, as did the many divorces among your acquaintances that did not leave you unscathed.

You are equally right to point out that—unnoticed by many—we are seeing a shift emerging in society. There are a growing number of young people who are simply fed up with utterly uncommitted cohabitation, notorious adultery, "marriage on the go," and the many other models concocted by the authors of countless sitcoms and trash novels. Instead, firm commitment and long-term partnerships are highly valued again. The marriage model of the previous generation no longer appeals to them. Above all, they no longer want their ideas of partnership to be driven by interest groups, whose lobbying work spills over into the media, university campuses, and government agencies.

This topic, however, is a vast field and I want to use this letter to expand a little on what I have said about the seven sacraments. It is important to me that the sacraments not be left standing isolated like erratic blocks in our lives but should work their way into everyday life. How can this happen? For this "continuation of the sacraments," the Church has a whole sequence of inconspicuous signs and rituals, some of which I want to list in what follows.

You certainly will have noticed that many of the faithful, as they enter a church, dip a finger into a small basin at the entrance and make the sign of the cross with the holy water*. Many do so simply to ask for God's blessing. There are Christians, though, who do this deliberately to remind themselves of their baptism, when they entered the Church and received a share in Christ's death and resurrection. I personally find this little reminder of crossing oneself with holy water to be theologically very fitting and beautiful. It must not fall by the wayside, due to intellectual arrogance that deems this "just popular piety."

Making the sign of the cross* is a similar ritual. You can do this in the morning when you get up or in the evening when you lie down to sleep. You could also start a difficult work assignment with the sign of the cross. Or you could make the sign on your child's forehead as they go out to school or get into bed at night. Obviously, the same applies to your spouse. This has nothing to do with magic but is the living, daily enacted remembrance that salvation exists only in the cross of Christ Jesus.

Another ritual that more Christians practice than one might think is the daily examination of conscience. You set aside some time when you are alone for a few moments and use that time to reflect on what you have failed to do in the preceding hours, where you might have hurt others, but also what good you have received. Finally, you think of God and ask forgiveness of God. Obviously, there is a connection between the examination of conscience and the sacrament of penance. The daily examination of conscience is a preparation for confession and brings it to life and fruition.

Is there also a good daily ritual that connects you with the Sunday Eucharist? Certainly! Maybe there is a church or chapel near your home that you might pass every day or can reach without taking a long detour. It can be very peaceful to stop by for a few minutes, direct your view toward the altar, the sanctuary lamp* that burns in front of the tabernacle*, calm down, and open your heart to Jesus Christ.

There are numerous other such symbols and rituals that remind us of the sacraments and that can transform our day. Naturally, the annual celebration of a wedding anniversary is also part and parcel of this. I wish with all my heart that soon you might be able to celebrate the anniversary not only of your civil marriage, but also of the sacrament of your Church marriage. Incidentally, canon law offers the possibility of having your marriage, which you entered out of love and with clear precepts, recognized retrospectively as a Christian marriage. This way, a formal wedding is no longer necessary, but the Church would simply grant its approval of the civil marriage you concluded long ago.

We can look at this in more detail sometime, but meanwhile, cordial greetings and many thanks for your kind letter!

Letter 37

LIFE FROM THE HOLY SPIRIT

Dear Paul,

My last letter addressed the idea that the sacraments must not be like lonely islands scattered into the life of a Christian. Instead, the entire Christian existence after baptism has a sacramental structure and is integrated into the coming of God's kingdom as it is a constant encounter with the Risen Lord.

Alas, such a life, lived wholly out of baptism and the sacraments, seems humanly impossible. And it *is* impossible for human beings because God always grants it anew. Yet we are given much more, because we encounter Jesus Christ not only in the sacraments but also in Holy Scripture.

This duality is very nicely explained in the divine Christian liturgy. When you attend Mass on Sunday with your wife and Anna, such a divine liturgy is more than just the Eucharist. It begins with the so-called Liturgy of the Word with a reading from the Old Testament and the recitation of a psalm* and a corresponding antiphon*. This is followed by a reading from the apostolic letters

185

of the New Testament and then a text from one of the four Gospels. This in turn is followed by the homily, the congregation's recitation of the Creed, and the intercessions for the Church and the entire world. Now I know that all this is familiar to you. I just wanted to list them in sequence.

We must distinguish between the Liturgy of the Word and the celebration of the Eucharist. However, these two parts of the Mass constitute one organic whole and complement each other, because we encounter Christ in the word of the *Scripture* and in the *Sacrament*. This is also why our entire life should have a sacramental structure and at the same time be permeated by God's word. Now you would be right to question a lofty expression such as "permeated by God's word." What does this mean in concrete terms, and how could this work?

Put very simply, it will only work with joy in the Holy Scripture. How does one attain joy in such an enormous book? Joy in something is the result of dealing intensively with it. I, for example, take great joy in changing landscapes. Woods interspersed with fields and meadows, the view from the mountains over the wide expanses of the land with the clouds passing by overhead, or the streams meandering through the countryside. How do I nourish such joy? By going on hikes.

Much of this holds true for Holy Scripture. One needs to explore it and learn how to engage with it. When I was twenty-two years old, I read the entire Bible from start to finish. Now, I would not advise you to do this to start, as such a project is akin to the extreme sports that some undertake. They take the direct route between two points and, disregarding rivers and gorges, mountains and glaciers, stick to a straight line as the crow flies to navigate all obstacles in their way. True, discovering a landscape and territory this way is exceptionally alluring and exciting, and one can explore routes that cannot be found in any travel guide. But by the same token, the undertaking is not without its dangers and requires suitable equipment.

So I do not recommend that you and your wife venture into the Bible in such a direct fashion. Why don't you start by reading Luke's Gospel and the Acts of the Apostles, because the two were initially one piece of work? You could follow this with the Gospel of Matthew, then an exploration of the Old Testament with the Book of Genesis. These are all shorter sections that are easily managed by the nonexpert.

Of course, you'll have to find the time, and if you find that time wanting, there is another possibility. Take selected Bible quotes for every day of the year. The internet is full of many such sites. You can also get a tear-off calendar with dedicated sections, often just a sentence for every day that you read in the morning and take with you during the day. This portions the Bible into manageable bits, which has its advantages but also disadvantages. It is a bit like taking a cable car up a mountain. Though the view is stunning, you miss out on the effort of climbing to the mountain top.

I am sure you understand what I mean. I have nothing against cable cars or extreme cross-country hikes, but to start, I recommend keeping the hikes to feasible distances. You will make your own discoveries along the way. Thus, you will find out that the Bible contains abundant richness in different narrative genres. It has stories, sagas, tales of the patriarchs, family trees, lists, laws, instructions, fables, parables, satire, psalms, songs, love poems, gospels, letters, prophecies, admonitions, lamentations, petitions, thanks, and prayers.

This multitude of genres, which are more or less absent in the Qur'an, not only make for plenty of variety but also reflect the huge spectrum of experiences that back up the Bible. Israel was like a laboratory in its encounters with God. Israel listened, watched, opened itself to God, but also locked itself up, closed its ears, rebelled, and turned away from God. Israel cried out and lamented to God, implored incessantly, thanked God, and recounted God's deeds, made itself the mouthpiece of creation so that all these emotions and manners of speech are reflected in the many different linguistic genres. The Bible is based on the continuously reexamined, corrected, expanded, and perpetuated experiences of centuries.

And the Bible is based on doubt, criticism, consolation, devotion, the search for understanding God's will, and the battle for the truth. The Bible knows aberrations whose course is corrected again, bitterness that is replaced by patience and hope, and doubt that is answered by certainty. The Bible is a huge, wild, and frighteningly beautiful book that reflects Israel's travails and struggles for the right life and right manner of living before God. It is a never-ending dialog with God, which makes it so exciting.

Naturally, it also contains segments that we cannot understand at first reading and at which we even bristle. If you see them as part of this unremitting struggle of the people of God to discover God's will, however, even these darkest chapters can reveal themselves to us.

Paul, you will already have noticed that I have no ready-made recipe for you on how to live with the Bible. It would be impossible. All I want to do is to kindle your love for this book and your explorative zest, interest, and persistence. The Bible really is God's word to us, albeit written entirely in the media of human words and texts. Only in Jesus did God's word become fully and eternally revealed to us, and it is right in our midst. If we do not take the long and arduous path that Israel had to take to arrive at Jesus, we today cannot arrive at Jesus either.

Heartfelt greetings to you, Anna, and your dear wife.

Letter 38

LIFE FROM THE COMMANDMENTS

Dear Beth,

My letter that preceded the last one, which covered life in the sacraments, resulted in an intense discussion between you and your husband. At issue was the baptism of your husband and the Church recognition of your marriage. You yourself are all for it. You can imagine both sacraments, and you are obviously also thinking of Anna, while your husband is still reluctant. If he prefers to receive baptism in peace and quiet and outside a parish service, I do not consider this a problem and would recommend such an approach for a Church marriage. The alternative— the retroactive Church recognition of your marriage— would in any case take place quietly. This approach would provide you, Beth, with the possibility to receive holy communion. But I am all for letting the issue rest for a while so that your husband can decide in all freedom and with the necessary time.

This letter's topic, "Life from the Commandments," could really be a theme for a Jewish rabbi because life lived by the commandments, or, more precisely, life lived out of the Torah, plays a crucial role in Judaism. There is even a specific feast for it, known as Simchat Torah ("Joy in the Torah"). Over the course of a year, the Jewish divine services read out the entire Torah, and Simchat Torah is the day of the last passage (Deut 33—34) and at the same time restarts at the beginning (Gen 1—2). This way the Torah reading never comes to an end. On the day of Simchat Torah, as many members of the congregation as possible participate in the reading, and in many synagogues the faithful dance around a Torah scroll or with a Torah scroll in their hands.

Now one may ask, Is it possible to rejoice over laws and legal stipulations? Apparently, as the faithful Jews do just that and the Israelites in the Old Testament already did likewise. In the Psalter*, Psalm 119 is one of the longest psalms, and it is nothing more than a meditation on how precious and pleasant the Torah is. Allow me to quote just a short section from this sheer unending song of praise for God's divine commandments:

> I run the way of your commandments,
>   for you enlarge my understanding.
>
> Teach me, O Lord, the way of your statutes,
>   and I will observe it to the end.
> Give me understanding, that I may keep your law
>   and observe it with my whole heart.
> Lead me in the path of your commandments,
>   for I delight in it. (Ps 119:32–35)

This is the way an observant pious Jew heeds and follows the commandments of the Torah from morning to night and orients his entire life to God. This orientation is no burden but becomes a joy in God.

Can a Christian live simply like a Jew does out of the Torah? Surely not! The Christian lives out of Jesus. In baptism a Christian has been united with Jesus Christ, and Christians live out of the faith in the crucified and Risen Lord. This faith frees Christians from all sin and guilt, heals them, saves them. This also explains why this letter was preceded by the letters addressing the sacraments, because faith and sacraments are inseparable.

We must state clearly that Jesus is not opposed to the Torah. He neither abolishes it nor replaces it. He fulfills and perfects it, which means he reveals its intentions and focuses on its core. This is exactly what Paul means when he states that all commandments are subsumed in the commandment to love (Rom 13:8–10). A Christian can equally rejoice in the Torah as in the other writings of the Old Testament. A Christian should not only know them but love them.

One of my last letters mentioned the daily examination of one's conscience. Such examination is related both to "walking the way of the Commandments" and to taking joy in the laws of God. Anyone having difficulty examining their own conscience will find that many Catholic hymnals contain helpful guides and suggestions. There's no need to follow these literally but they can certainly be thought-provoking. The following examination of conscience, which a good friend of mine formulated, may offer inspiration:

Do I believe in God's grace? Do I believe that God leads and carries my life if I let it happen?

Do I trust God that something new can happen in my life, or do I not believe in resurrection to a new life in faith?

Do I follow only my own thoughts and ideas, or do I believe that God can speak to me through other people?

Is my life just made up of habits that I determine, or am I willing to have my life transformed for the sake of the gospel?

Do I take pleasure in the mistakes of others because they make me appear superior?

Have I tried to compensate for the weaknesses of others, or have I rested on them and used them for my own ends?

Do I care for the lives of others, or am I utterly indifferent to them?

Do I fearlessly allow clarity about my life, or do I hide behind half-truths and lies?

Do I trust in God's grace, even in suffering and matters that I cannot yet understand today?

This would be a slightly different and very personal form of examining one's conscience. Nonetheless, it should be clear that examination of conscience is not just limited to capital sins, such as murder, adultery, theft, fraud, or defamation. Our life with God and our life out of God's commandments is woven together much more finely and more subtly. And yet the small things are often what can lead us to or away from God. What's more, adhering to and fulfilling the commandments in the small things of everyday life can give us quiet joy that no one can take away.

I greet you all with my heart.

Letter 39

LIFE OUT OF PRAYER

Dear Paul,

My last letter with the comments about examination of
conscience triggered some doubts in you as you wonder
whether this does not actually cause one to dwell on sin.
This can depress us so that in the end we might be left with
a despondent feeling of low self-esteem, for whom every
joy in life and the world has been destroyed.

Indeed, this can happen, "under certain
circumstances," if a person's nature is predisposed to
depression and self-reproach. In this case, good pastoral
advice would recommend other spiritual exercises.
In normal circumstances, though, an examination of
conscience and confession are uplifting, grant peace, make
us realistic, and can help us to be grateful. So I want to use
this letter to address gratitude because it is the deepest root
of all our prayers.

We are created by God, and the reason for our sheer
existence is solely based on God's will and love for us. Yet,
God did not just create each one of us alone but created an
entire world around us that abounds with causes for daily
joy: mountains and valleys, air, clouds and water, flowers,
animals, and humans, night and day. I sometimes recite in

my heart the poem by Lothar Zenetti entitled "Footing the Bill":

> One day we will be presented
> with the bill
> for the sunshine
> the rustling of the leaves,
> and tender lilies of the valley
> and the dark fir trees,
> for the snow and the wind,
> the bird flight, the grass and the butterflies,
> for the air we have breathed and the gaze into the stars
> and for all the days,
> evenings and nights.
> One day it will be time
> for us to set out and pay
> the bill please.
> Yet we've counted out the patron,
> who says "It's on the house"
> with a smile that stretches out
> to all the corners of the world:
> "It was my pleasure!"

Those signs of creation to which Lothar Zenetti alludes are not everything, because aren't we ceaselessly destroying all the elements he lists? As we discussed earlier, this is the reason why God initiated a counternarrative against our destructive fury in the history of the people of God. So we also must be deeply grateful for this history and have this gratitude turn into a prayer.

The way you love your wife with all your heart, Paul, must not be hidden away deep down in your heart. Your love and gratitude must come to the fore and reach out to your wife; it must speak up, express itself, and find the right words. The same holds true for prayer. The most important prayer is the prayer of thanksgiving and, connected to this, the praise of God.

Of course, not every day does the sun shine or do the lilies of the valley bloom. Nature also knows pain, the destitution of peoples, and the Church knows hardship. That's why there are supplications and lamentations. Does this surprise you? They do exist, and lamentation before God is a true prayer. For example, such a lament could say, "I fail to understand all this, O God. Why do you let it happen? Why don't you interfere? Why do you torment us so? Can't you see what is happening in the world?" These lamentations are true prayers, but if they are borne out of faith, they will soon switch over into pleas: "Help us and end this affliction! Make us see what we can do! Save your people and bless your legacy!" The psalms are full of such lamentations, but time and again they transform into intercessions and gratitude.

There is yet another form of prayer, which may be the ultimate and most profound form. It is quiet, silent prayer, in which we simply hold up our life to God and without much ado say, "You alone are holy, you alone are the Lord. All glory to you in all eternity." This is what the Church calls "adoration."

Obviously, there is so much more I could say about prayer. But does God need our prayer? Does God need our adoration? Of course not! But we need the prayer so that we may live a dignified human life and fully become what we are. Everything we are we owe to God. By praying to God, pleading, begging, and thanking God, we live out what we are: God's creatures.

The prayer of supplication is also something that could merit a lot more explanation. Does God help me only because I plead with him so incessantly? Or are things completely different? Does God not always want to help, and am I not always in the dominion of God's care and love?

I merely need to open to God's helping love, which is exactly what happens during prayers of supplication. Strictly speaking, my supplications do not change God, but they change me so that I can open up to God and he can act in me.

Paul, I had wanted to show both of you that when humans understand who they are, who God is, and what humans owe to God, we humans cannot live otherwise but in prayer. It becomes second nature, the breathing of our souls. And anyone who no longer breathes....

I am fully aware that the issue of prayer will never be conclusively settled and there's always so much more to say. But I need to close now and wish that you would just try it!

As always, with the best wishes to you all!

Letter 40

THE OUR FATHER

Dear Beth,

You are full of indignation over the latest act of Islamist terrorism in Spain, where a truck was driven into a crowd of people, and you ask me, "What kind of religion begets such crimes?" You are also fully aware that most Muslims would never do such a thing and fully reject these eruptions of violence.

At the same time, we must not overlook the fact that the Qur'an and the prophet Muhammad's teachings present a constant problem. Neither the Qur'an nor Muhammad nor Muslim tradition draw a clear line between the state and religion. Instead, they favor the idea of a state that basically does not recognize freedom of religion or merely tolerates it in limits. Those who consider freedom of religion to be something deeply aberrant will easily be tempted to attack outsiders and those with different beliefs.

Equally problematic is Islam's stance on violence. The Qur'an contains passages that encourage and incite violence, and Muhammad himself led his followers into many battles. Due to these circumstances, there are always factions within Islam that want to install a theocracy and propagate violence against all non-Muslims in the name of their religion.

In contrast, the New Testament and the early Church are unequivocal on this and draw a clear line between the people of God and the state. These are two utterly distinct entities that must not be mixed (cf. Matt 22:21). The state authorities hold the sword because they must secure order within society (Rom 13:1–6). The people of God, on the other hand, are committed to nonviolence. If later centuries witnessed acts of violence within the Church (e.g., forced conversions or the persecution of heretics), then these were clearly in violation of the Sermon on the Mount (cf. Matt 5:38–48) and indeed against everything Jesus lived and taught.

This can be seen in the Our Father, which I had wanted to say a few words about in this letter. In the fourth supplication of the Our Father, we pray, "Give us this day our daily bread." Unfortunately, this version of the fourth petition does not fully convey what we read in Matthew 6:11 or Luke 11:3. This version of the fourth petition that is customary in the Church seeks to combine Matthew's and Luke's renditions. In Matthew we find the most original source, where it says, "Give us this day our bread for tomorrow" (cf. Matt 6:11). What is one to make of this strange request?

It becomes comprehensible only if we put ourselves in the situation of the disciples at the time. They are traveling with Jesus through Israel to proclaim the kingdom of God. In the morning they do not know where they will find shelter for that night. Nor do they know if anyone will give them food to eat. That is why they pray for bread for the *coming day*, which in the time calculation of those days started the evening before. Thus, they pray with this petition that they may find hospitality in a house where they will be fed. It means that they are not to plan ahead; they are to make no preparations, carry no provisions, be unafraid of the future, but only care for "today" (Matt 6:34).

We know even more about the situation of Jesus's disciples. Not only did they travel without provisions (Luke 9:3), but they carried no tools and above all no weapons with them. Not even a stick or spare clothing could they take with them (Matt 10:9–10). Unlike the Zealots* (the Jewish religious warriors of the time), they are to proclaim the kingdom of God through absolute nonviolence. This is what Jesus had wanted for his disciples.

Please excuse me, Beth, for having taken you into these specific questions of the interpretation of the Our Father, but these are questions of huge significance. They demonstrate that Jesus absolutely ruled out the use of violence. His messengers were to travel without money, weapons, or any equipment. This was to signify that God's kingdom comes without violence and can be accepted only in freedom. Anyone in Church history who violated this stood against Jesus.

The very same mind-set of Jesus is evident in the fifth petition of the Our Father: "Forgive us our trespasses, as we forgive those who trespass against us." "Trespassers" are those who were against Jesus's disciples, who wronged them, inflicted harm on them. The disciples are asked to forgive them and reconcile themselves with them. In another section we hear Jesus say that one must reconcile with those with whom we do not live in peace as soon as possible and under any circumstances (Matt 5:23–25). The Our Father gives the following reason for this: God also forgives the disciples all their sins and trespasses. At least they can ask God for this forgiveness, but obviously they must then extend it toward others.

In this same context I can also cite the second petition of the Our Father. It pleads for the coming of God's kingdom: "Your kingdom come!" What kingdom is that? It is certainly not a theocracy, in which the state decrees the religion and in which culture, society, and religion are identical. The kingdom of God that Jesus proclaims is rather the arrival of a world in which peace and reconciliation dominate, carried and supported by a sharing among people who want to serve God in complete freedom and without violence.

So you see that this fundamental text of Christian faith, the Our Father, ranks as a clear commitment to complete reconciliation, freedom of faith, and nonviolence. The disciples whom Jesus had sent out and to whom he taught the Our Father trust that there are people willing to accept in freedom the gospel of the coming kingdom of God. The disciples also trust that in the evening they will be received into the houses of friends and sympathizers, where they will be fed, until they move on the next day to proclaim God's kingdom somewhere else.

They not only place their trust in these other people willing to help them but also trust in their Father in heaven. They consciously and deliberately address him as their "Father" at the beginning of this prayer. This is what Jesus had taught them. The word *Father* holds a lot of meaning and speaks of the deep trust that the one for whose sake they even left their own families will now take good care of them. They are to be as carefree as the "birds of the air" and the "lilies of the field" (Matt 6:25–34).

I have now written at length about the Our Father and, of course, we who say this prayer today no longer travel like Jesus's disciples to proclaim the kingdom of God. Nonetheless, we are bound to this prayer and we are supported by it. We are given to live out of the reconciliation, just as we are given to trust our Father in heaven in everything. In our shared lives we are never to resort to violence. And every time we say the Our Father, we beg that the kingdom of God may come for the entire world, so that there will finally be peace among nations.

The Our Father

Now I must explain two further small details of the Our Father. Let's start with the sixth petition: "Lead us not into temptation!" How can God lead us into temptation? The answer really is quite simple if we take *temptation* to read the same as *testing*. God can lead humans into a situation where they are tested, because our faith must prove itself, grow, and strengthen. God led Abraham into such a situation (Gen 22:1), and so was Israel tested in the desert (Deut 8:2). So all those who want to follow Jesus must prove their faith (Rom 5:3–5). But God will not lead us into a test, says the sixth petition, that is beyond our power and that the disciples could only fail.

What are we to make of the first petition: "Hallowed be thy name"? In the ancient world of the Middle East, the "name" stood for someone's reputation, their authority, their dignity, honor, and respect. Whenever the people of God quarrel among themselves, when they live in violation of the gospel, when they are unreconciled and violent, the good "name" of God is disgraced and even destroyed, because how else could God's name be great and hallowed in the world if not through the people God has chosen in the world so that his will would be done among all people?

Beth, you might have sensed already how much goes into this short prayer, which we Christians are permitted to say on the instruction of Jesus. It is a prayer with a wide and very far-reaching horizon, and it wells forth from the depths of history. Its roots are the mission of the disciples two thousand years ago. Yet we too are permitted to say it, and say it for the glory of God, the coming of his kingdom, and the credibility of his people. If we say it, this very prayer that Jesus had entrusted to his disciples may even become our home.

I wish you and all your family such a home in faith
and in prayer from my whole heart.

Letter 41

"GLORY BE TO THE FATHER"

Dear Beth,

I'll come straight to your first question: I simply do not know whether the authoritative leaders of Islam might one day cease to place religion and the state on the same footing. Nor do I know whether they will one day come out clearly and unambiguously in favor of freedom and nonviolence in matters of belief. I hope so, of course, but I simply don't know, because the Qur'an is just not like the Bible, which is "God's word in human words," but is considered as literally inspired by God.

Moreover, the fact that Muhammad used violence, in stark contrast to Jesus, is historically irrefutable. Jesus allowed himself to be killed rather than incite violence among his disciples. Thus, Jesus tells Peter, who tries to liberate him during his capture, "Put your sword back into its sheath!" (John 18:11). This is the measure Christians can follow, and the Sermon on the Mount is equally unequivocal.

There is another problem on top of this. What actually *is* "Islam"? Where does it speak with one clear and

202

unambiguous voice? The Catholic Church has its teaching office: the pope, the bishops, its councils, all of whom interpret Holy Scripture and Church tradition when addressing crucial questions of faith. Where does Islam have this clear and unambiguous interpretation?

Your second question is much easier to answer. No, you need not keep in mind everything that I said about the meaning of the Lord's Prayer in my last letter when you recite the Our Father. You can say it very easily and simply by placing all your trust in God, the heavenly Father. There is no need to have the disciples wandering through Israel before your inner eye as you recite the petition for bread.

You may also think of what the Church needs today and what your family needs. I think you understand what I mean. You don't have to stick to the letter when praying but should open your heart to God. Only occasionally will you have to remember the actual words of the prayer.

But now on to your third question. You were browsing through the New Testament again and came across a sentence Paul uses in his First Letter to the Thessalonians (5:17): "Pray without ceasing!" Now you ask with some sense of irritation, "How can that work?" Allow me to try to formulate somewhat more bluntly what you are trying to say: "I have my husband, my daughter, a job, and a house to attend to. With all that and my job as an administrative assistant, I must remain levelheaded. How can I possibly pray without ceasing?"

My answer is "You can!" Paul does not mean that you are constantly muttering prayers but that there are short moments during your day when you can lift up your heart and think of God. There are many such opportunities.

You can look out the window in the morning and see the sunrise. You can take joy in putting on a new sweater. You'll have a few moments to reflect while stopped at traffic lights or waiting for your computer to start up. You find yourself at a loss for words when writing. You have just met somebody who gave you a kind, heartfelt smile. Sunday lunch turns out to be a real treat, as you can see from the happy faces around you. I could go on forever.

Every day holds enough such moments when we can say a short prayer of thanks or petition. Those around you need not even notice. And there are always many occasions to take joy in God, lament and cry to him, beg, implore, praise, and maybe even sing to God. I will also name a prayer that you can recite from time to time. It goes, "Glory be to the Father and to the Son and to the Holy Spirit, as it was in the beginning, is now, and ever shall be. Amen."

This is a very old prayer that dates all the way back to the fourth century. It is a confession of the triune God: praise of the Father, who created us, of the Son, who liberated and redeemed us, and of the Holy Spirit, in whom the Church lives. At the same time, it seeks to have this praise carry and fulfill our entire existence. It should never end and one day will be our entire salvation. I myself say this short praise many times during the day and hope that I will also be able to do so in my hour of death.

By the way, when I pray alone, I use the following formula: "Glory be to the Father through the Son in the Holy Spirit." This variation expresses even more poignantly than the classic formulation that Father, Son, and Holy Spirit revealed themselves to us in real history and that they do not merely coexist unrelated to one another but are one communication into which we are integrated.

Dear Beth, how wonderful that we can share our thoughts on prayer!

Please extend my kindest greetings
to the entire family.

Letter 42

THE COMMUNION OF SAINTS

Dear Paul,

Many thanks for your letter and for talking to your wife about prayer. It is indeed not so easy to integrate such a new element into everyday life and the routine of a family.

I'll delve straight into your question regarding the icon of Mary, which Anna was given for her birthday two days ago. Of course, you should hang up the icon. It seems to be an old and valuable piece, and as you write, your aunt's gifts are never kitsch. Your problems are in any case not aesthetic ones but refer more principally to Catholics' veneration of Mary. Why, you ask, does Mary play such a big role? Is Catholicism in the end subconsciously *worshiping* Mary? Could she be a surrogate for the grand maternal goddesses of the old pagan world?

First, as I learned as a child in Sunday school, Mary is not *worshiped* but *venerated*, though this obviously does not really answer your question. Why is there such veneration of Mary in the Catholic Church in the first place?

Put very simply, the Church wants to take seriously the sentence from the psalm that Mary prayed according to Luke 1:48: "Surely, from now on all generations will call me blessed." Mary, however, is not called blessed because of her own power or importance but because "the Mighty One has done great things for [her]" (Luke 1:49). Of course, the veneration of Mary has also seen exaggerations and misapplications. Yet the background to it all is based on the simple fact that she is the mother of Jesus.

If I have a good friend, I will honor and respect his mother as well. Should it be any different in the case of Jesus? However, much more is at stake.

According to the account provided in Luke 1:26–38, Mary answers the angel's message with, "Here am I, the servant of the Lord; let it be with me according to your word." Though we need not take this account as strictly historical, the sentence "let it be with me according to your word" does not need to be fixed at a specific point in time. What we should do is take this sentence seriously as a statement on Mary's existence, otherwise we would miss the truth of the Bible. Mary must have offered, with her entire existence, a pure, wholehearted, unreserved yes to God's will. She must have made herself a "servant" of God all her life. Mary married herself to the will of God, even as this will remained obscure and dark to her, and even as this will turned into a sword that went right through her soul (Luke 2:35). If her yes had been a hesitant, half-hearted yes, God's eternal word could not have become human within her.

This gives Mary a key role in the history of our salvation, for her yes made Jesus Christ possible. We are deeply grateful to her for this, and we view her as an image of the faithful people of God and as the epitome of the many in Israel who had pinned their hopes on God's definitive and final act.

All of what I have said just now changes nothing in the way that we worship only God and glorify God alone. We are not alone in this but do it together with Mary, in deep gratitude to God for giving us this sister and mother.

At the same time, the question carries substantially more weight and implications than suggested at first glance. I recently read the following from a Protestant theologian: "We have to say an unequivocal 'No' when Mary, the mother of Jesus, is elevated into the role of an intercessor, helper and mediator. As the children of God, as sons and daughters of God, we may and must pray *directly* to God, the father of Jesus Christ." What are we to make of this?

Of course, all Christians can and should pray "directly" to God, the Father. There is no question; it is self-evident to every Christian. But it is only a half-truth: what is missing here is the view of the whole person, human history, and all that makes humans what they are. From the very first second of our existence to our death, we are dependent on others, as I have already said in an earlier letter. We depend on deputies, surrogates, and representatives who help us in the slow process of becoming human and existing as human beings. This applies not only to our physical existence but also to our faith. Though the faith is God's gift, pure grace, it still is *transmitted* and handed down to us by our predecessors, parents, persons we've met, and ultimately the Church. We have many intermediary representatives, also in the faith.

It is a basic tenet of human existence to "live by representation," which one could philosophically also call "coexistence" or "partaking." This is how God willed us to be. We are not lost, lonely souls, whose relationship to God could be adequately summarized in this sentence: "God and the soul, the soul and its God." The whole Bible, all of salvation history, reflects this constant representation.

Abraham, Moses, the prophets, Mary, Jesus. For without Abraham, without Moses, without Israel's long history with its countless believers, Jesus would not have been possible. That is why they are all an integral part of our faith, and that is why Mary is also an essential element of our faith.

When we discussed the triune God, I pointed out that we are only a "person" in the full sense of person through our relations to countless other human beings. Our being a person is constituted by the web of "relations" to others. Some of these others have already passed away, but the relationships to them remain and are part of our life. Church tradition calls this highly complex web of links between the living and the dead, who support one another in the faith, the Communion of Saints.

Intercessory prayer to the saints, then, is simply the distillation of a fundamental constant of faith. It is nothing less than the conscious realization of the gift we have been given in partaking in the faith of Abraham, the faithfulness of the prophets, the example of the saints, and the yes spoken by Mary.

Protestantism was right to stress "God alone," "Christ alone," and "grace alone," because popular piety is always in danger of falling back into simple religion. At the same time, Protestantism pushed aside, painted over, or partly forgot a basic constant of human existence that the Catholic tradition has always held: A life before God and faith in God, and hence also prayer, only ever exists in the "together," the interweaving of the many representations and surrogates. After all, we can pray to God the Father only "through Christ and with him and in him," as the eucharistic doxology* states and as Paul wrote (see Rom 1:8; 7:25). So here already we have intercessory mediation.

Of course, when we pray, we need not constantly remind ourselves that we now do so "through Christ." However, from time to time we should remember this—

liturgy* does all the time. Every classic oration* ends in the formula: "through Christ, Our Lord." This was only the most important and central example to show that our prayers are always "mediated." In the case of Mary, much of this holds true on another level, even though it is not exactly the same.

So, in what sense is Mary a "mediator"?

Certainly not in the sense of a receptionist who decides whether someone is allowed to see her boss. Neither does she fit into the category of "friends" who facilitate things. Instead, Mary takes up a central position in salvation history for having spoken the yes that we all have to say to God if we believe. And we can say this yes only if we enter into *her* yes. So in this sense she is also a mediator, mediator to Jesus.

For the same reason, Mary is not just the mother of *Jesus* but also our dear mother, and that is why we can ask her to intercede for us with her Son. We find an example of this intercession in an old Christian prayer that goes back to the early Middle Ages. Its first part is all biblical, bringing together the salutation of the angel to Mary during the annunciation (Luke 1:28) and the greeting Elizabeth speaks to Mary (Luke 1:42). A few centuries later a concluding plea was added to this first biblical part:

> Hail Mary, full of grace,
> the Lord is with thee.
> Blessed art thou among women,
> and blessed is the fruit of thy womb, Jesus.
> Holy Mary, Mother of God,
> pray for us sinners, now and at the hour of our death.
> Amen.

It is a wonderful prayer, very plain, humble, and realistic. *One does not have to say it as a Christian*, but one is free to say it. It places us amid the large Communion of

Saints, and it concludes very realistically with a view of our end and the hour of death. I want to make this view of death my next topic.

Many greetings to you, your wife, and Anna. And please be so kind and forward my belated birthday greetings! (Oh dear, that constitutes as another act of surrogate mediation!)

Letter 43

WHAT COMES AFTER DEATH?

Dear Beth,

How are you all doing? I did not receive an answer to my last letter because you are presumably on holiday. So I'll just continue with my letters because I feel the urge to conclude my walk through the big issues of Christian faith. My last letter ended with the Hail Mary, and this prayer is in turn a look at death. Is it not remarkable that we think of our hour of death every time we recite this prayer?

Death is once again a topic that receives more reflection today than in the past, with many women and men deliberating on what a dignified death could be. They are acutely aware of their own deaths, and with their relatives go through the motions of what could happen in cases of progressive dementia or prolonged coma. Others do volunteer work in the hospice movement.

Having said all this, though, what happens "afterward" does not receive much attention. Here the mental suppression of old continues unabated. For many it is utterly alien to think about what comes after death. They don't ask themselves this question but rather suppress it whenever it crops up. That is strange because so infinitely much depends on its answer.

If death were to be followed by an absolute void, the big questions of our life would forever remain unanswered. More though, the countless innocent victims of rape and of torture to death, those annihilated from history, would never have their life and honor restored. And the brutal suppressors that keep plundering, tormenting, and denigrating others would be right. We would then live in an absurd world.

Only the biblical faith in the one and only God, who judges, sets right, and restores the dignity of the lowly and suppressed, can really give a true answer to this question.

Another completely inadequate answer is the idea of many of our contemporaries living on after death in their children. Of course, it is true that the good we have done lives on in those who come after us. Sadly though, so does the evil we have done. Nor does this answer the question about the rights of the raped and oppressed who lived in the centuries *before* me. To them, the answer that the good *I* have done continues to live on in my children is of no help whatsoever.

Equally inadequate is the notion that we continue living after our death by being reborn again and again through reincarnation*. Such a concept does absolutely no justice to the seriousness of our existence. For if my life is but a long sequence of reincarnations, I can decide anew time after time, I can overturn every decision, and I never have to really commit myself to anything, as I still have infinite possibilities for self-optimization. Though this is in keeping with today's arbitrariness and fear of commitment, it is also a contradiction of the human essence. Our dignity lies in precisely the fact that we can commit ourselves,

stand faithfully for what we have discovered to be right,
can decide here and now for the good and just cause,
and thereby give the world a better, kinder face. This we
cannot and must not postpone indefinitely.

Finally, the idea shared by many today that they will
dissolve and become one with nature or the cosmos is
utterly inadequate. As if their lives' energy could flow forth
into flowers, trees, and many other life forms, indeed even
reach out into the cosmos or some kind of universal cosmic
consciousness. Can you really keep a straight face when
you read this as a perspective on the future of a human
being: "You will be the purring cat, the tree whose leaves
rustle in the wind, the stone washed over in the riverbed,
the star in the skies, the blond shine in the hair of a
wonderful woman living a thousand years from now"? We
can find this message in ever new iterations of countless
New Age works.

Let's get serious and look at it earnestly! In view
of the solution just presented, one should at least ask:
Hasn't the biological and cultural evolution of humanity
developed in the opposite direction, to an ever more
acute awareness, a liberation from mere instincts and
urges, to emancipation from the overpowering dictate
of the collective, toward personification and ever deeper
understanding of the irreplaceable nature of each human
individual? Human development is not heading toward
a loss of all individuality but toward recognition of others
as persons and toward becoming more and more a person
oneself. Human beings are made for encounter, and this
is the very goal toward which human beings have been
heading for centuries.

This is why only faith in the Bible does justice to
human nature. It is the faith that believes that in death we
will encounter God, who is person in the highest sense of
the word and not some diffuse cosmic energy. In our death

we will encounter God, and thereby also ourselves, wholly and completely, for the first time. My next letters will address this in more detail.

I greet you all from my heart and
in our shared Christian hope.

Letter 44

FACE-TO-FACE WITH GOD

Dear Beth,

Still no news from you! This is very unusual, but what can I do? I'll just continue. As I wrote in my last letter, "Human beings are made for encounter." What's more, they are made for encountering the living God, who created them, keeps them alive, guides them, and lavishes them with graces. In death we will finally meet and encounter this God.

The word *finally* is crucial in this context, because even now we encounter God in myriad ways. We encounter him in the joy and need of our prayers. We encounter him in our church services, in which we try to look up to him and express our gratitude to God. We encounter God in every service we offer someone else and in every good conversation that we engage in with other human beings.

Yet in all these encounters God remains hidden from us. It seems as if God is silently and constantly retreating from us. We can never hold on to him or claim to have recognized him. We are forever setting out anew to reach

215

him and must start out anew with him. We meet God in many ways, but never come to an end with him. That indeed is the biggest problem in our prayers: that we speak into a perpetual silence. While our prayer is meant to be a dialog with God, our conversation partner seems to be silent. I say, "seems to be," because in reality God does answer us, sometimes instantly, sometimes later, often in minuscule signs one easily overlooks. God does indeed talk to us, yet the hidden seclusion remains.

In death, though, we will finally encounter God, the God of our prayers, our longings, our hopes, and our faith. So when we speak of "heaven," we are not referring to any nice things awaiting us there, but "heaven" is nothing else than the encounter with God himself. God will then shine before us, but how this will be, no human being can describe. At most, we can think of the times in our lives when we were suddenly overcome, and the scales fell from our eyes so that we could recognize the connections and relations of which we had no inkling before. Or we will recall those moments when we would have loved to say with Goethe's Faust, "Stay a while, you are so beautiful." These are moments that are full of splendid bliss but that pass by far too quickly.

Yet even these comparisons are ultimately fruitless undertakings that must pale compared to the real encounter with God. In our death we will meet the eternal God, and then we will understand and grasp how close God has always been to us, even in those hours when we thought him far away. We will then recognize how mighty and holy God is, infinitely greater and holier than the image we made of him. God will shine before us, great and holy, so that from then on, God will consume all our perception, thinking, and being, finally and forever.

When seen from such a perspective, I find the term *eternal rest*, which Christians use to describe life with God, somewhat questionable. Meeting God is everything but "eternal rest." It is unfathomable, breathtaking life. The Catholic Church cherishes the established tradition of praying for the dead, for example, with the words:

> Eternal rest grant unto them, O Lord,
> and let perpetual light shine upon them.
> May they rest in peace. Amen.

Both terms, "rest" as well as "perpetual light" are solidly biblical (cf. Isa 60:19). The background to these images of "eternal rest" is mostly the rest Israel enjoyed when it finally entered the promised land and all prophecies were fulfilled (cf. Deut 3:20). But "rest" can also be misunderstood as meaning exhaustion, sleep, deathly silence, standstill. This, however, is exactly what is *not* meant. I have privately modified this old intercession for the dead and pray, "Lord, grant them the eternal joy of Easter!"

Be that as it may, all of this is just imagery. We, however, can say with Paul that we shall see God "face to face" (1 Cor 13:12). Against such a vision, all the images and experiences we have ever made will fail.

I think of you and greet you with all my heart.

Letter 45

JUDGMENT

Dear Beth,

I finally found out the reason for your extended silence. You simply could not get yourself to write. I am deeply sorry to read what you wrote in your last letter. For the first time in your marriage, you are experiencing a crisis, in which neither of you understands the other. The carefree interaction between your husband and yourself, for years a matter of course, has suddenly come to a halt. You cannot talk or communicate with one another anymore, and Anna is devastated.

The point of contention that triggered this situation continues, and I can't give you any advice on it. I am in no position to assess how important the professional position that your husband has so surprisingly been offered actually is. Nor can I judge what it would mean for *you* to have to give up your job, sell the apartment you inherited from your parents, and move to a region that would also be completely new for Anna. Least of all can I comment on the alternative your husband suggested, in which he would be absent during the work week and return home only on Saturdays.

But it is important for the two of you to communicate with each other again. You cannot let the situation fester to the point where you just ignore each other. Again, I am in no position to offer any well-meaning advice, but I hope and pray for a solution. Meanwhile, I'll just continue with my letters and you need not answer them.

The last thing I wrote was about encountering God in death, which will be an unfathomable and totally overpowering encounter. The unholy, guilt-ridden human being and the holy God: This encounter will turn into judgment. When we meet God in death, we will discover in all clarity who we are in reality for the first time.

God has no need to sit in judgment over us. God does not have to speak to us as human judges speak to the accused. God does not need to tell us where we have failed abysmally, where we deserve chastisement, where we are guilty. He does not need to judge us.

There will be no judgment in this sense of the word. The encounter with the holy God will open our eyes about ourselves and we will recognize who we truly are. We will not only encounter God but for the first time in our lives be clear-sighted about ourselves. We ourselves will then pass judgment on ourselves and condemn the evil within us. The encounter with God will turn into self-judgment.

When theologians speak today of judgment in death or the so-called Judgment Day, the term *self-judgment* plays a vital role. God does not judge "from above" or "from outside," nor does God punish us. We ourselves become our judgment and punishment.

Surely it is insufficient to say that in the presence of the holy God, we pass our own judgment on ourselves, because we also pass this judgment on our "victims," who inexorably come into our field of vision at our death. They are the many we failed to help, though we could have, the many we could have consoled and did not comfort, the many to whom we could have been an image for the faith and utterly failed, and all those we overlooked, disappointed, embarrassed, disregarded, misused for our own ends, led astray, or seduced. All of them will appear before us in death and will look at us. And they too will become our judgment. We must even assume that when we meet our victims during judgment, we will have to relive all the suffering we inflicted on them.

So the encounter with God in death will become an encounter with the truth: the truth about God, the truth about the world, and the truth about ourselves. In this sense, we can hope for judgment, because truth is something to look forward to. I myself hope that all the dark corners of my life will have light and clarity shed on them, so that I will find out, for example, what I had really wanted in life deep down. I hope whatever is vague and dubious will assume clear contours, that the muddle of guilt and innocence will be untangled, the really good becomes visible and the ambiguous clarified, the only seemingly good be uncovered, and the evil within me revealed. I hope that all the centrifugal forces, the scattered and disparate debris of my life, will be gathered and brought home.

Such clarification of the all-pervading truth of God must be something very liberating, and probably it is this very clarification that reveals God's unfathomable mercy. I will write about this mercy in my next letter.

Dear Beth and dear Paul, please don't be alarmed that after all these years of living so naturally side by side this crisis has befallen you. Something good could come of it, if you treat each other mercifully and ask God for his help and true insight. Be patient with one another!

I greet you full of hope and confidence.

Letter 46

THE MERCY OF THE JUDGE

Dear Paul,

In the Old as well as the New Testament it is often said that God judges the world in righteousness. In fact, the entire Bible is permeated with statements about God as a strict and punishing judge. It even contains expressions referring to "God's anger." How does that fit with God's mercy?

We need to establish what the Bible means by this anger. In view of the injustice and evil in the world, God cannot simply look away. Evil is attacking God's creation and attempting to destroy the world. Far more, God cannot let injustice in the people of God go unanswered. After all, Israel was to be God's tool to help the world. Therefore, God must act to establish justice, and that is meant by the term "God's anger." It is the *exasperated anger of the judge* who seeks to establish justice and wants to restore the world.

In addition, the Bible can say that God's anger is not permanent but subsides, and God's compassionate mercy "grows warm and tender" (Hos 11:8). This reversal from

anger into mercy, from judgment to salvation, speaks out
in many texts in the Old and New Testaments. Thus, God
answers the infidelity and rebellion of his people with
faithful loyalty. His heart beats for Israel and he has to
show mercy for his people. In Isaiah 54:6–8 we read the
metaphorical analogy of the people of God being like a
woman and wife:

> For the LORD has called you like a wife forsaken
> and grieved in spirit, like the wife of a man's
> youth when she is cast off, says your God. For a
> brief moment I abandoned you, but with great
> compassion I will gather you. In overflowing wrath
> for a moment I hid my face from you, but with
> everlasting love I will have compassion on you, says
> the LORD, your Redeemer.

There are numerous other Old Testament texts I
could quote that show God's wrath turning into mercy.
Jesus knew all these texts and indeed considered them
foundational. Though Jesus also announced the impending
judgment, as the prophets had, the basis of Jesus's
message is the proclamation of abundant and overflowing
redemption. The parable of the prodigal son (Luke 15:11–
32) has Jesus defend his behavior toward those who have
failed, not only in their faith, but in their entire existence.
Jesus goes up to them and takes them into the new events
happening in Israel, just as the father in the parable does.
The prodigal son does not have to atone for his failures,
does not have to toil as servant to recoup his squandered
inheritance, but his father reinstates him instantly with full
rights as son, and a feast is celebrated.

Paul, it would be nice if you read this parable once
more—after all, it is one of the greatest parables in world
literature—perhaps together with your wife. I think I
had already recommended this in an earlier letter. Above
and beyond all stories and history, can God really act

any differently from the way Jesus describes the father's reaction in this parable?

And could it be that Jesus demands an unlimited will to forgive, an unconditional and boundless readiness to reconcile as the proper conduct in the people of God, only for God to then fall behind such reconciliation? So when Peter asks, "If another member of the church sins against me, how often should I forgive? As many as seven times?" Jesus answers him, "Not seven times, but, I tell you, seventy-seven times" (Matt 18:21–22). This means always, without any bounds and preconditions. As Jesus is the definition of God, his image, the reflection of God's nature, what are we to make of this?

We can put our trust in meeting a merciful and compassionate God in our death. The grace of God not only accompanies our life, but it will truly reveal itself the moment we finally encounter God, when our eyes are opened, and we have to recognize our own merciless cruelty. At that very moment, God will meet us like the merciful father in the parable of the prodigal son. God will not probe us with questions of guilt and justice, but God will draw us close to him in infinite joy. Such will be the real experience of our death as we behold God's love, grace, and mercy.

I greet you both full of confidence.

Letter 47

UNITED WITH THE RISEN LORD

Dear Beth and Paul,

Late yesterday night your long message arrived, and what a surprise it was! You told me in detail how the hard knot finally unraveled. I was always certain, right from the start, that the two of you would come together again. I was equally certain that your daughter Anna would come to play the lead role in this. Back when she insisted on baptism and first communion, she set things in motion, and she has done it again. You should be grateful for this daughter!

Paul, I don't think you will be losing anything. On the contrary: you have won much more. Your crucial sentence was "My family is more important than my career," and this will prove to be a blessing. In fact, it already has, as not only you but also your wife have found that things have moved on. You took a step toward your wife, and she had to understand and did understand that your renunciation of professional advancement was by no means a foregone conclusion. It was indeed a very consequential decision.

These kinds of decisions often show only afterwards that they were right. Then, however, this becomes obvious, as you write, "This conflict has changed both of us. We are as much in love with one another as we were ten years ago, but now it is different and actually nicer. Isn't that strange! There must be hidden synapses between our souls, as we both, spontaneously, felt that we wanted another child."

Good enough! Let me continue the topic of my last four letters in which I tried to outline what happens to each one of us in death: We encounter the living God. And this encounter turns into our judgment. It becomes a judgment because we come face-to-face with God's full love. It is only love, the purest and self-giving love, that gives us the strength to see ourselves in the right light and allows us to be transformed in the light of God. You yourselves experienced this over the last few days.

To everything I have said about encountering God in death, I must add one more remark, a crucial one. If I have so far written of death as an encounter *with God*, I did so for the sake of simplicity. This was, however, shorthand, which I now finally need to set right. In death we will encounter not simply God but also the Risen Jesus.

For everything I have said about a human being's final encounter with God is expressed in the New Testament in the same way as an encounter with Jesus. Our death is the magnificent definitive encounter with him, and he will appear to us as the Crucified One. As the Crucified One, he will judge the world in power and glory, for he is God's justifying grace. Jesus will grant us eternal life, transforming our mortal body into the glorified figure of his body. This is what the New Testament says of Jesus Christ.

Is this then a "parallel," juxtaposed existence of God and Jesus in these final events? No! Because if we look closely, we will have to conclude that we encounter God *in Jesus Christ*, for in him God will shine before us. We will see God's face in Jesus's face and in the encounter with him we will experience God's judgment. It is in him that God will grant us his redeeming mercy, and in him we will be taken into the life of the triune God.

If one asks why, over and above the straightforward statements made in the New Testament and in tradition, the only answer is this: because it was already so in history. Often and in many ways, God spoke to the fathers, but his final, definitive, and irrevocably enduring word was spoken in Christ Jesus (Heb 1:1–2). In Jesus, God attained final openness and presence in this world. In Jesus, God said all there is to say about himself and fully bound himself to the world. In Jesus, God's loving yes to the world and to humanity was revealed finally and forever. From then on, anyone who wanted to know who God was had to look at Jesus. Those who saw him saw the Father. Those who encountered him encountered God himself (John 14:6–11).

If Jesus is then the place where God's self-communication has definitively entered into our history, and if earthly history does not simply run its course in the beyond but finds its lasting finality into which everything of significance in earthly history enters, then Jesus Christ will also be the true place of our encounter with God in the hereafter of all history. He will then be in all eternity what he was already here on earth: the one in whom we are granted life; the one in whom God speaks the eternal word of his love.

Maybe the deepest and most beautiful mystery of the Christian faith is that God has accepted humankind so unreservedly. God so loves the world that we will encounter God in all eternity in no other way than in the one who became human flesh. And therefore, forever and always, we will find God in the heart of a human being.

I greet you full of joy for all that has occurred between you and all that you are planning. I truly understand you!

Letter 48

CREATION FULFILLED

Dear Paul,

You have inundated me with questions, mostly about purgatory*, the resurrection of the body, and, of course, hell. I do not know where you got all these catchphrases, surely not from Mass? From the internet, maybe? (I know that you research frequently and eagerly.) No matter where these questions come from, I will try to answer them in what follows.

As far as your question about purgatory is concerned, I have basically already provided an answer at an earlier point, as one of my last letters had addressed the judgment. I had noted that in death, the unholy human being stands before the holy God or, to be more precise here, comes face-to-face with Christ. This, however, means the unreserved and complete disclosure and clarification of everything a human being carries in them. Anyone who can take a sober look at themselves knows how much ambivalence, self-justification, self-assertion, and self-indulgence they carry with them, as well as fear, mistrust, harshness, and self-deceiving lifelong lies. All of this is laid bare, revealed, purified, and transformed in the light of Christ's love, and this is extremely painful. At the same time, it is carried through by the joy of being with Christ. I had called it "self-judgment" and had written that all those whom we hurt during our lifetime, in death will come to stand before us and we will have to suffer their suffering with them. All of this is our purgatory and our purification.

As this cleansing purification is not bound by earthly timeframes, it is natural that the basic decision taken by the person concerned well before death should be oriented toward the good, truth, the other human being, and ultimately God.

Next, you inquired quite justifiably about the resurrection of the body in the flesh. Now *flesh* in the meaning used here is certainly unusual. When we hear *flesh* we think of either the butcher or a beach full of sunbathing bodies. In the Bible, though, *flesh* means more than just *body* or physical body parts. It can designate the human being as such, everything it is, its entire existence. In our context the biblical formulation "all flesh" is important as it refers to all of humanity or even all living creatures. "All flesh" shall bless God's name, says Psalm 145:21. And in Joel 2:28, we read, "I will pour out my spirit on all flesh." This emphasis can certainly also be understood to refer to humans' fallibility, their weakness and transience. Still, what is meant is the whole human being with everything that characterizes and is attributable to that person.

"Resurrection of the flesh" then means that all humans, all peoples, all cultures, will appear before Jesus Christ, the judge of the world. What happens during that judgment I have already outlined as the revelation of all that has happened, the good and the bad. It is clarification, purification, transformation, and, finally, taking part in the life of the Risen Lord.

The New Testament says significantly more on this. Not just everyone and all nations will appear before and be judged by Christ. In Romans 8:18–22, Paul speaks of the groaning of "creation itself" and "the whole creation." So not only human beings, but entire nations are groaning and sighing. All creation together with humanity is groaning in birth pains. This means that nonhuman creation is also waiting for liberation and redemption, awaiting "the revealing of the children of God" (Rom 8:19). This means to say that, together with humanity, all of creation waits to take part in Christ's paschal glory.

The New Testament thus speaks of a tremendous hope, which holds that the Risen Christ partakes in the glory of the Father, and all who believe in Christ and love him partake in the resurrection of Christ. Even nonhuman creation will partake in what is to happen to human beings. I will not even think about trying to expound on this. We cannot.

All we can do is to start from the creation of the world. Though God has called everything into life and constantly keeps it in existence, his creation must have an aim, a goal. To say God willed into being the cosmos, the world, humanity, history, and the evolving cultures, only to let them all fall back into nothingness, is absurd. God created all of it to guide it to perfection and to its destiny. This destiny is to bring home all of creation into the resurrection of Jesus and thereby into the eternal life of God.

It is at this very juncture that you quite rightly ask about hell. Would God's creation not be a mistake if in the end there were people who had to live in eternal distance from God and hence in infinite suffering for all eternity?

This question is even more pressing, as the New Testament does speak numerous times of hell, although it mentions God's will for universal salvation far more often. God "desires everyone to be saved and to come to the knowledge of the truth" (1 Tim 2:4), so God wills salvation for all. Can God succeed in this? And what if someone does not want salvation?

Let us assume that there is a person who does not want the good, but evil, who wants evil precisely *because* it is evil. Someone who does not want truth but lies and lives such lies right down to the core of their existence. Or someone who says, "I am enough for myself. I am my own meaning and purpose. I want only myself and nothing else."

If this person existed, a person only ever on the lookout for themselves in all the principal decisions of their existence and in complete denial of everything else, God would have to leave that person to themselves and to their own locked-in-themselves existence. After all, God cannot overpower such a person and will certainly not force them. Such a person would then truly have only themselves, and that is exactly what hell would be.

One can only hope that such a person does not exist. One can only hope that God's grace will prove victorious even over such cases by breaking open the self-erected prison of that person's existence before they die. So one can only hope that hell is empty or, to put it differently, that no one turns themselves into hell. Yet such statements are only an expression of pure hope. We simply do not know.

Hell remains a terrible possibility, which is why the Bible speaks of it. Anyone wanting to banish all talk of evil from the world, the horrors humans are capable of, and our self-created hells will not make the world a brighter or more human place but will merely obscure its depths. For talking about hell opens our view of the far-reaching and consequential decisions we make every day. It shows us how we just allow evil to take its course in the world, how we close our eyes to suffering, injustice, and violence—or how we can work against the evil within ourselves and in society, with patience and the spirit of the gospel.

Talking about hell is necessary for the sake of the sober and realistic view we must take of history.

Talking about hell is necessary because of the tremendous responsibility we hold.

Yet this talk of hell must always be set against a far heavier counterweight: God's absolute will for salvation.

I find it hard to end this letter to the two of you with the topic of hell. You will surely have noticed, however, that the word *hell* is really something quite different from what we normally associate with it. It really is a matter of our responsibility for the world. We cannot just look on, as people hate, injure, defame, and destroy each other, but we must take a stand and act. We can do so by following Jesus, and we can do so in the Church, which is Jesus's dwelling in the world.

Kindest heartfelt greetings!

Letter 49

THE MEANING
OF EASTER

Dear Beth and Paul,

To wrap up my thoughts on death and what will happen to us in death, I want to say something about Easter. You will quickly see why.

Years ago, I heard a preacher say, "Easter means that for us too, life will go on after death." This sentence shocked me. Is it true that our lives "continue" then, just with the slight difference that need and suffering will end? As if we were to continue living after death, just in better surroundings? Is that resurrection?

No, this is not what the New Testament means by *resurrection*, as it does not constitute a continuation of life under better conditions. Instead, resurrection is preceded by a real end, by death. This means that things don't just go on. Death means the end. Death means it is over. The story of our life breaks off. If we are not unequivocally clear on this, we cannot understand the miracle of resurrection. For resurrection means that death is vanquished, but it still is that very *death* that is being vanquished.

The Meaning of Easter

Christians as well as Jews take death very seriously and do not trivialize it. This is the reason for the darkness of Good Friday* with its grief and its misery. This is why the mother of God cries as she holds her dead son in her arms, grief-stricken. This is why there is a grave into which the bloodied and slain corpse of Jesus is laid. This is why the Apostles' Creed contains the sentence: "He descended to the dead," and this is why there is no liturgy on Holy Saturday*.

No, resurrection does not mean that things will continue as before, hour after hour, day after day, and year after year. On the contrary, resurrection means that our lives have truly come to an end, but that the Risen One takes our entire life, the way we lived it, into his eternity.

In Christ God resurrects our entire life, the whole history we lived through, from conception to death, all days of our life, every hour that we believed, hoped, and loved. Nothing is lost.

Resurrection is the harvest of our life, and everything there was is collected, gathered, and brought together by God. Because of this, every hour that we live right now has an immeasurable weight.

Every praise of God that passes our lips today becomes eternity, and every smile we give someone else becomes eternity. Every affliction we bear in patience and humility will be transformed into joy by God. Every hour of our life that we used to help others in the faith and to build up community will become a treasure never to be lost again.

What we live, right now, in this very hour, has tremendous weight, because what we haven't done cannot rise again. So doing the right thing has a tremendous significance. *What, then, are we to do?*

To start, we could simply read the Easter accounts in the Gospels. Here it says that the Risen Lord appeared before his disciples and showed himself time and again to them. Strangely enough, though, when he did appear before them, he never spoke of the bliss of eternal life. The Risen Lord never said to his disciples, "Rejoice for I have risen and therefore you will also rise. Look forward to everlasting life!" The words he did speak to his disciples, all and without exception, have the goal of *sending* them out, so that they might bear witness to what they heard and saw. Thus, the Gospel of Matthew ends with the words of the Risen One:

> Go therefore and make disciples of all nations, baptizing them in the name of the Father and of the Son and of the Holy Spirit, and teaching them to obey everything that I have commanded you. And remember, I am with you always, to the end of the age. (Matt 28:19–20)

The appearances of the Risen Lord, then, are not about instructing the disciples about eternal life, but about telling them to set up, all over the world, communities of disciples that live according to the Sermon on the Mount.

This is all that matters, that people should be won over to the gospel and should live it. Most people will believe in Jesus's resurrection only if they can see with their own eyes that his resurrection is already transforming the lives of Christians now.

For this reason, hope in the resurrection can never mean staring into the heavens and forgetting about earth, but it means being there for others, building up community, and witnessing the gospel to other people. This is also why the miracle of the resurrection of the dead begins, not at the end of time, but every Sunday. It begins right in our midst, if we cast off our fears, open our lives to the others in the community, help them, and serve them.

Beth, your last letter contained some sad news, informing me that your previous parish priest is retiring and moving to another diocese*. He is being replaced by

a priest from another continent, who is still struggling
for acceptance in the parish community, as the language
barrier makes his way of expressing himself unfamiliar
and foreign to many parishioners. That was the sad part of
your letter.

Now for the second part, the good part in your report.
You and your husband could not accept such an attitude,
so you and the Williams family have banded together and
extend invitations to the new priest at regular intervals.
Every week now you check his sermons for language that
is easy to understand and grammatically correct, encourage
him, and help him where you can. I must say that I was
extremely happy to read what your two families have set
in motion, as other parishioners have begun to join you.
It was like the "joy of Easter," and so I want to take up
this "joy of Easter" to call an end for now to my "teaching
letters."

We had started with your request to help you get
to know the Christian faith better. This was not easy for
me and I often found writing quite an effort. Without
your cooperation these forty-nine letters (so far) would
have been impossible. I thank you with all my heart for
everything you have given me over these many weeks: your
exceptional openness and deep trust. Please keep on the
path that you have set out on with Anna!

Let us remain connected in heartfelt friendship!

Letter 50

THE DARING OF FAITH

Dear Anna,

A little while ago I suddenly realized that I have written many letters to your parents and none to you. I can't let this stand; it is simply not right. So this letter goes to you.

At first sight it seems that I know very little about you, as I do not even know what you like to do, what your interests are, whether you like to read books, for example. (I myself was a real bookworm at your age.) And finally, I don't even know what you look like.

At the same time, I know something very significant about you, the fact that you decided for yourself to receive first communion together with your friends. That also meant that you had to have yourself baptized first. Your parents wrote this to me, and it really impressed me.

I myself was unable to make such a decision, as I was baptized as a little baby and so have absolutely no recollection of my baptism. When I was eight, I received my first communion, which was also not much of my own decision. I just did what the others also did. Now you at your age have already decided to take a step that was important to you. For me, such important decisions came much later in life.

Of course, you will also have to make more decisions in life. And faith is also something you must win over time and again. It is nothing cheap, that you can just acquire. All the great and wonderful things in life are always a daring adventure.

You know that your parents are also facing up to such a daring venture right now, as your father is considering being baptized and accepted into the Church. Nothing seems to have been decided yet, and everything is still open.

However, your parents are making a true effort of getting to know the Christian faith, for which I greatly respect them. They are doing so very thoroughly and have asked me question upon question and then discussed my answers. They have even started to read Holy Scripture regularly and are making every effort to grow into the life of your parish. I am convinced that the two of them will do the right thing.

Dear Anna, you can be very grateful for your parents. They are God's gift to you. You should be forever grateful for having them, because not everybody has such parents.

> I wish you strength and endurance for your service
> at the altar, but above all joy in your faith,
> as I greet you very cordially.

> P.S.: If you ever want to write to me,
> I would be really delighted.

GLOSSARY

Abbot: From the Latin *abbas*, which in turn is derived from the Aramaic *abba* (father). The abbot is the superior of a community of monks. The corresponding female is the *abbess*. According to the influential Rule of St. Benedict, an abbot is elected by the monks (chapter 64). During Church history, this right to elect the abbot has at times been partly curtailed or even abolished by external intervention.

Abram / Abraham: The Bible initially calls Abraham "Abram" (Abram = "my father is exalted"), which probably referred to the protective deity of the affected person, so that it means "My protective deity is exalted." There are various names that include the word *God*, such as "Dorothee" (goddess's gift), Deusdedit (God gives) or Amadeus (loved by God). Genesis 17:5 then changes the name "Abram" into "Abraham," which means "Father to the many (people)." Abraham is also the first of the three biblical patriarchs Abraham, Isaac, and Jacob.

Altar server: Children, adolescents, or adults who undertake certain tasks during Mass in the Roman Catholic Church. During solemn Masses and high feasts, they carry candles or dispense the incense.

Antiphon: A refrain or verse that can be recited or sung repeatedly. A beautiful example from the Old Testament is Psalm 136. The original purpose of the antiphon was to incorporate the entire congregation in the singing of psalms.

Apostles' Creed: A confession of faith that says, "I believe in God, the Father almighty, Creator of heaven and earth, and in Jesus Christ, his only Son, our Lord, who was conceived by the Holy Spirit, born of the Virgin Mary, suffered under Pontius Pilate, was crucified, died and was buried; he descended into hell; on the third day he rose again from the dead; he ascended into heaven, and is seated at the right hand of God the Father almighty; from there he will come to judge the living and the dead. I believe in the Holy Spirit, the holy Catholic Church, the communion of saints, the forgiveness of sins, the resurrection of the body, and life everlasting. Amen." While the formulation of this old confession of faith does not originate with the twelve apostles, its constituent parts do largely go back to New Testament times. In its form it is an expansion of the ancient Roman confession of baptism. Because the original time and place for reciting the Apostles' Creed was during baptism, the prayer does not contain all the faith's tenets, such as Jesus's proclamation of the kingdom of God. And the word *catholic* does not carry the later denominational relevance but stands for "general," "all-encompassing," and "universal." The phrase "resurrection of the body" is not a literal translation from original sources but should instead read "resurrection of the flesh." The Apostles' Creed can be recited in place of the Nicene Creed during the celebration of the Eucharist.

Atonement: In the Bible atonement is a salvific event that originates with God. Atonement granted by God interrupts the connection between sin and the sphere of evil that surrounds every sin. The New Testament says that Christ atoned for our sins, which means that he gave us the chance of a new beginning. The biblical term for atonement thus means something different from what we generally understand by atonement. Usually we take atonement to mean that the human being who has become guilty must reduce this guilt through some sort of equalizing compensation that is to be rendered or served, as, for example, with a fine.

Bishop: From the Greek *episkopos* (overseer). In the Catholic Church the office of bishop is the highest level of the sacrament of ordination. Normally a bishop oversees a diocese and sits as member of a national bishops' conference and in the synod of bishops. In the Catholic Church, the bishops are seen as the successors to the apostles.

Breviary: A collection of the texts, hymns, and prayers that comprise the Liturgy of the Hours, which priests and religious pray at specified times throughout the day.

Catechism: A handbook or reference that teaches the key elements of the Christian faith. It explains primarily the Apostles' Creed, the Ten Commandments, the sacraments, and prayer.

Chalcedon: Ancient port city that today is part of the city of Istanbul. In AD 451, it was the site of the important ecumenical (i.e., "encompassing the whole Christian world") Council of Chalcedon.

Chapter: In the context of this book, the gathering of members of a monastic community who vote on various matters as defined by the rules or constitution of their order.

Chasuble: The outer vestment worn by the priest during the celebration of the Eucharist. The color of the chasuble—white, red, green, or purple—corresponds to the liturgical season or celebration on the church calendar.

Christ: From the Greek *christos*, literally, "anointed one." In ancient Israel, kings and high priests were anointed with oil when appointed to their office. The king for whom Israel longed at the end of days was known by the name of "The Anointed," or in Hebrew, *mashiakh*, Messiah. "The Christ" therefore means "The Messiah." In the Church, "Christ" was from the start one of Jesus's most important honorary titles.

Christmas: Christmas Day on December 25 is one of the Christian Church's most important feasts. It is the day the Western Church celebrates the birth of Jesus Christ, even though the actual chronological date of his birth is unknown.

Christology/Christological: The theology concerned with the person and work of Jesus Christ.

Collection (of alms): During the celebration of the Eucharist, a plate, basket, or bag is passed around the congregation to collect alms for the parish or charitable work.

Communion: From the Latin *communion*, meaning "fellowship/community," referring to the union we have with Jesus Christ when receiving the Eucharist. As Paul writes in 1 Corinthians 10:16: "The bread that we break, is it not a sharing in the body of Christ?"

Confession: Often refers to the sacrament of reconciliation, with all its constituent parts such as examination of conscience, repentance, confession of sins, absolution, and eventual restitution. *Confession* can also mean the part of the sacrament when one tells one's sins to a priest.

Constitution: Some texts of the Second Vatican Council use the term *Constitution* for solemnly ratified documents of varying legal force. One of the most significant is the Dogmatic Constitution on the Church (*Lumen Gentium*), promulgated in 1964.

Council: An assembly of Catholic bishops from throughout the world, which, under the leadership of the pope, consult on urgent issues of faith and Church life.

Deacon: From the Greek *diakonos*, meaning "servant, helper." In the Catholic Church the diaconate is the first level in the sacrament of ordination. Deacons have the authority to proclaim the Gospel during Mass, to preach, and to administer holy communion. They may also administer baptism and preside at church weddings and funerals.

Diocese: A geographically defined district of Church administration overseen by a bishop, also known as a "bishopric." It is subdivided into parishes. At present there are approximately three thousand dioceses in the Roman Catholic Church.

Doxology: Celebratory praise of the triune God, usually at the close of a prayer. For example, the Eucharistic Prayer at Mass ends with the doxology: "Through him [Christ Jesus], and with him, and in him, O God, almighty Father, in the unity of the Holy Spirit, all glory and honor is yours, forever and ever. Amen."

Easter: The most important feast in Christianity, celebrating the resurrection of Jesus. Every Sunday recalls this "first day of the week" (Mark 16:2) and, as the "Day of the Lord," is like a small Easter feast. Liturgically, Easter is celebrated over a fifty-day period, characterized especially by the word *Alleluia*. Pentecost marks the end of the fifty-day Easter season.

Easter Vigil: The culmination of the Triduum, celebrated at the end of Lent on the evening before Easter Sunday. In this liturgy, the Christian community congregates to celebrate Jesus's resurrection from the grave as well as their own resurrection. The Easter Vigil begins in darkness and is then lit by the new fire and the Easter candle, which symbolizes the Risen One. Each congregant receives a candle lit from the Easter candle. The "Exsultet" is a festive hymn of praise of the Easter candle and the mystery of that night. During the vigil seven readings from the Old Testament can be read, particularly the story of the exodus from Egypt. The high point of the celebration of the word is the Easter Gospel followed by the blessing of the baptismal water, after which the congregation renews its baptismal vows. This is followed by the festive celebration of the Eucharist.

Encyclical: An encyclical is a circular letter addressed to many readers. In the meaning particular to Catholicism, it is a teaching document from the pope and addressed either to all bishops in the Church or, on rare occasions, to all people of the world, as was Pope John XXIII's peace encyclical *Pacem in terris*. Papal encyclicals are usually written in Latin and named by the first two or three words.

Eucharistic Celebration: In the Catholic Church the eucharistic celebration is often referred to simply as "Mass." The "celebration of the Eucharist" can be used to refer to the second part of Mass, beginning with the preparation of the offerings. "Celebration of the Eucharist" is also used to mean the entire Church service.

Eucharistic Prayer: The Eucharistic Prayer is the central part of the Mass. It follows the preparation of the gifts with a dialog between the officiating priest and the congregation: "The Lord be with you."—"And with your spirit."—"Lift up your hearts."—"We lift them up to the Lord."—"Let us give thanks to the Lord our God."—"It is right and just." This dialog conveys the significance of what happens next, the celebratory giving of thanks by the entire Church for what God has done, and thanksgiving in particular for the work of Christ. In the midst of this thanksgiving (*eucharistia* in Greek), the Holy Spirit is invoked on the offerings of bread and wine, and Jesus's Last Supper is remembered. Through this thanksgiving remembrance, Jesus becomes present in bread and wine. The Eucharistic Prayer ends with a solemn doxology.

First communion: In most countries, first communion is usually received between the ages of eight and nine. First communion is usually communally celebrated with the parish congregation, although exceptions can be made.

Good Friday: The Friday before Easter, that is, the Friday of Holy Week. The adjective *good* signifies "holy." On this day, the Church commemorates Jesus's death on the cross.

Heavenly kingdom: Also "God's kingdom." In Judaism the word *God* was and is often paraphrased in formulations like "the Name," the "Holy One," or "the Heavens." Unlike the evangelists Mark and Luke, Matthew consistently and with only four exceptions uses the term "kingdom of heaven" rather than "kingdom of God."

Holy Saturday: This is the only day on which the Catholic Church does not celebrate a Mass, as it commemorates the period when Christ is at rest in the tomb.

Holy Water: Water that has been blessed by a priest with a prayer to remind the faithful of their baptism. In addition, like all blessings, it expresses the idea that all creation is blessed by God.

Israel: In this book, every mention of *Israel* refers to the biblical Israel and not to the modern state of Israel.

Laity: Formerly used to designate the faithful, who held no Church office. The Second Vatican Council has widened this understanding. It speaks of the great mandate bestowed on all the faithful, who on the strength of their baptism and confirmation alone are already sent out to give witness of the gospel. By according the biblical concept of "people of God" a new meaning, the Second Vatican Council realigned the previously sharp juxtaposition between the laity and Church officials.

Liturgy: From Greek, where it referred to public service. Accordingly, the liturgy is the official and public divine service of the Church, in contrast to private prayers or devotions. The central but not sole form of liturgy is the celebration of the sacraments, above all the sacrament of the Eucharist. The precondition for all liturgy is God's self-revelation in history, which is why, in many places, the liturgy recalls God's deeds. In the sacraments, God's salvific deed in Jesus Christ becomes immanently present and is answered with praise.

Magnificat: Mary's prayer of praise on the occasion of her visit to her relative Elizabeth, found in Luke 1:46–55.

Mass: The most important form of the Church's divine service is the Mass, consisting of the Liturgy of the Word and the Liturgy of the Eucharist. The word comes from the Latin *missa*, meaning "dismissal, discharge." Initially referring to the concluding blessing and dismissal of the faithful, in the Middle Ages the word gradually came to mean the entire liturgy itself, indicating that the blessing the Mass bestowed was considered rather more essential and significant than the great thanksgiving to God.

Monotheism: The belief in a single God, which, especially in Israel, was asserted strictly by the prophets and theologians in the period after the Babylonian exile (see Exod 20:2–3). Before this time, Israel's practice was more a "sole veneration" of YHWH that still tolerated the existence of other deities. YHWH (pronounced "Yahweh") is the name of God in the Old Testament.

New Testament: Twenty-seven books of the Bible, containing the four Gospels, the Acts of the Apostles, twenty-one letters to Christian communities and associates, and the Book of Revelation. The New Testament constitutes an organic unit together with the Old Testament and forms the final, concluding layer of interpretation and meaning of the writings of the Old Testament.

Old Testament: The Bible is composed of the Old and the New Testaments, which together are an indivisible unity. The Old Testament is neither outdated nor superseded by the New Testament. *Testament* as such stands for the biblical word *covenant*. The "New Covenant" does not replace and supplant God's covenant with Israel but rather "renews" it and bestows an eschatological quality on it.

Oration: A short solemnly stylized prayer that the priest recites aloud. The Mass contains three such orations: the "prayer of the day" before the readings, the "prayer over the gifts" at the end of the offertory, and the "concluding prayer" before the final blessing. The orations are brief because after the invitation to pray ("Let us pray"), a pause should be inserted, intended for each member of the faithful to pray quietly for themselves. The subsequent oration is merely the conclusion and summary of the silent prayer of the congregation. Many orations are very old and real jewels of the old Roman liturgy.

Order: Church communities, either of men or of women, who lead a communal life (*vita communis*) and have dedicated themselves before God to a life of poverty, chastity, and obedience.

Our Father: Jesus himself taught his disciples this prayer, and it has reached us in two versions, in Matthew 6:9–13 and Luke 11:2–4. The original version prayed by Jesus can only be surmised. As far as the overall format is concerned, Luke is probably closest to the original source, while Matthew is more original in the individual phrases, especially in the fifth intercession. The Our Father gives us crucial insights into Jesus's will and lived practice. Here is the wording of the prayer: "Our Father, who art in heaven, hallowed be thy Name. Thy kingdom come. Thy will be done, on earth as it is in heaven. Give us this day our daily bread. And forgive us our trespasses, as we forgive those who trespass against us. And lead us not into temptation, but deliver us from evil."

Parish: Every diocese is subdivided into units called parishes, for each of which a priest has pastoral responsibility. The system of such units has developed over time, and the parish sizes are contingent on historical and local conditions. Alongside the territorial parishes there are also personal parishes such as student communities.

Paschal Lamb: The Jewish Passover feast includes eating the paschal lamb, which has its biblical basis in Exodus 12:1–14. At the time of Jesus, paschal lambs were slaughtered in the temple. This meal of eating the lamb was called the Seder meal. It is probable that the Last Supper Jesus ate with his disciples was the Seder meal on the eve of Passover. In today's Seder meal, it is no longer customary to eat an entire lamb. The New Testament refers to Christ as the paschal lamb (1 Cor 5:7).

Passover: Jewish communities celebrate the Passover (Hebrew: *Pessach*) together with the feast of the unleavened bread over a period of eight days in commemoration of their liberation from Egypt. The Christian Easter feast is rooted in the Passover feast. See also the entry for "Seder meal."

Pentecost: The anglicization of the Greek word *pentekoste*, meaning "fiftieth day." Pentecost is celebrated on the fiftieth day of the Easter season. It is the celebration of the Holy Spirit descending on the disciples as described in the Acts of the Apostles 2:1–13.

People of the twelve tribes: The Old Testament describes Israel as a people of twelve tribes (Gen 49; Deut 33; Josh 4), named after the twelve sons of Jacob: Reuben, Simeon, Levi, Judah, Issachar, Zebulun, Joseph, Benjamin, Dan, Naphtali, Gad, and Asher (Gen 35:22–26).

Polytheism: A religious system that worships a multitude of gods. They often include one high or main god. In many polytheistic systems, the gods are not clearly distinct from the world but represent forces of nature or history.

Priest: Many religions have a priesthood, whose principal duty is to present the gods with sacrifices. Jesus and the New Testament communities kept a clear distance from this kind of priesthood, as Jesus's deeds meant fulfillment and hence also the end of all sacrifices (Heb 7:25–28). Thus, the Church's priests do not offer new sacrifices, but they are authorized to recall—to the presence in the Eucharistic Prayer—the one and eternal sacrifice of Jesus Christ. As they do so, they themselves represent Christ. Accordingly, the designations of offices in the New Testament communities were deliberately not taken from the cultic sphere (*episcopus*, elders, deacons). They are rooted in Jesus sending out the twelve disciples (Mark 3:13–19), a foundational act for the Church. Over the following decades they evolved into a fabric of ecclesiastical services that eventually structured itself into the threefold office of bishop, priest, and deacon, alongside additional functions. Delegated by the bishop, the priest's duty is to preside at the celebration of the Eucharist, proclaim the Gospel, and gather and guide the community.

Psalm: Originally a psalm was sung with the accompaniment of a string instrument. Many of Israel's psalms are compiled and structured in the Bible's Book of Psalms.

Psalter: Originally used to refer to an ancient Middle Eastern musical instrument, much like today's zither or hammered dulcimer. The meaning was transferred gradually to the "Book of Psalms" in the Old Testament, which includes the 150 psalms. These psalms can be any kind of prayer, whether lamentations, pleas, thanks, or praise. The "Book of Psalms" was certainly not a songbook for the divine service in the early Jewish synagogues and by no means the one used in the temple services (although it also contains songs, or portions of songs, that were once recited at that time). The Book of Psalms was instead used in more "private" early Jewish gatherings of the faithful, where it served as a book of meditation. Psalms can be found in other sections of the Bible as well, such as the Song of Victory at the Sea of Reeds in Exodus 15:1–18 or the Benedictus in Luke 1:68–79. The Church's liturgy often makes recourse to the psalms, and in the fixed prayer schedules for members of religious orders and priests (Liturgy of the Hours, Breviary) the Book of Psalms is foundational. Any book that contains all the psalms can be called a Psalter.

Purgatory: Since in death the unholy human being cannot prevail before the holiness of God, we must be purified through the encounter with God. This process of purification affects the entire existence and history of the affected person. Referred to as *purgatory*, from the Latin *purgatorium*, "cleansing," it is also the root of the word *purge*.

Reincarnation: *Reincarnation* can also be translated as "re-embodiment." Some religions, above all today's many New Age beliefs, hold that after death a person's soul or some other form of spiritual energy finds a new body (transmigration of souls).

Sanctuary lamp: The sanctuary lamp is a candle, usually encased in red glass, that burns day and night in the proximity of the tabernacle and symbolizes the eucharistic presence of Jesus Christ. As the tabernacle is often positioned in a side chapel, the sanctuary lamp is also a visual guide for those wishing to pray. This tradition goes back to the prophetic promise in Isaiah 60:19: "The sun shall no longer be your light by day, nor for brightness shall the moon give light to you by night; but the LORD will be your everlasting light, and your God will be your glory."

Secondary cause: The concept presupposes that God is the "First Cause" of all of creation. Though God keeps the world continually in existence, within the world so created by God, there are multiple secondary causes, which are described, for example, by physics or history. When a person acts, this action is a secondary cause. God can act as a first cause "through human beings" but never intervenes in the world directly and at a specific instance. God always acts through secondary causes, for otherwise God himself would make himself a secondary cause.

Seder: The Seder is held on the eve of Passover, or *Pessach*. During this highly ritualized meal, the entire family gathers to recall

Israel's liberation from Egypt. The biblical basis for the Seder is Exodus 12.

Sign of the Cross: Blessing oneself or others with the sign of the cross is an ancient Christian custom, reaching as far back as the second century. Initially the sign of the cross was made only on the forehead. Today the fingers of the right hand start out on the forehead, come down to the breastbone, and then touch the left shoulder and then the right to redraw the figure of a cross. While doing so one can speak the words "In the name of the Father, the Son, and the Holy Spirit."

Stole: Part of the liturgical vestments worn by a bishop, priest, or deacon, made of a double-sided length of cloth draped around the shoulders and hanging like a scarf. Deacons wear the stole draped from one shoulder across the body and clasped at the hip. The stole is worn underneath the chasable and is in one of the liturgical colors. In antiquity, the stole was a kind of shawl, which became more and more stylized and gradually evolved into a symbol of office.

Surah: A section of the Qur'an, much like a chapter. The Qur'an has a total of 114 surahs, with the longest at the front and the shortest at the end.

Tabernacle: A decorated box or receptacle used to store the hosts (consecrated wafers), the bread of the Eucharist, to keep it for distribution to the sick and dying as well as for eucharistic adoration. The word *tabernacle* comes from the Latin word for a tent or hut: *tabernaculum*. The biblical background is the tent for the ark described in Exodus 26—27 that accompanied Israel during the wanderings through the desert and that was considered a site of God's presence (Exod 40).

Torah: The Hebrew Bible is made up of three parts: The Torah, the Prophets, and the Writings. The Torah consists of the first five books of the Greek Bible: Genesis, Exodus, Leviticus, Numbers, and Deuteronomy. However, the word *Torah* also has other meanings. For example, in Judaism it can mean the Torah scrolls or the entire Holy Scripture. An apt translation of *Torah* would be "commandment" rather than "law."

Glossary

Trinity: Based on the Latin *trinitas* (tri-unity), meaning the Christian teaching of the triune God of a single God in three persons.

Wisdom (personified): The Old Testament often refers to Wisdom as a person: while created by God, Wisdom was present during the creation of the world as a kind of "blueprint." For more details, see Proverbs 8:22–36; Sirach 24:3–22; and Wisdom 7:22—8:1. In Israel's theology, personified Wisdom is soon equated with the Torah.

Zealot/Zealots: Jewish freedom fighters who were against the Roman occupying forces in Israel after the first century AD. They understood the first commandment to mean that God alone can be ruler in Israel and not the Roman emperor.